072383

391   Sichel, Marion
S   History of Men's costume.

072383

391   Sichel, Marion
S   History of Men's
        costume.

MAY 13
MAY 13   3000
MAY 19   8308
OCT 27   8558
AUG   9   3300
OCT 31   4000
NOV   1   15291
JUN 11   18690
JUL 26   17488
                               12688

HISTORY of MEN'S COSTUME

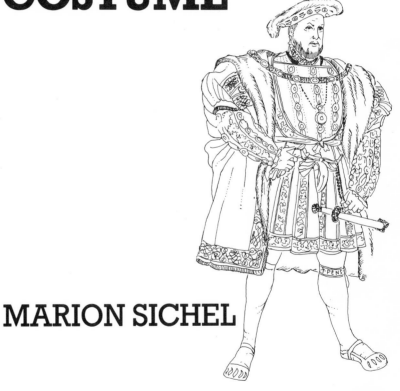

MARION SICHEL

Batsford Academic and Educational Ltd   *London*

Typeset by Tek-Art Ltd Kent
and printed in Great Britain by
The Anchor Press Ltd
Tiptree, Essex
for the publishers
Batsford Academic and Educational Ltd
an imprint of B T Batsford Ltd
4 Fitzhardinge Street
London W1H 0AH
                85 B9746
British Library Cataloguing in Publication Data

Sichel, Marion
    History of men's costume.—(Costume reference)
    1. Costume—History   2. Men's clothing—History
    I. Title   IISeries
    391'.1'09   GT1710

ISBN 0 7134 1513 4

Contents

The tailcoat has padded and puffed long sleeves. The pantaloons are worn with high boots with tops in a contrasting colour, c 1808

The man on the left wears a houppelande and on his head a hood-turban, known as a *chaperon*, with the hanging piece twisted up. The man on the right has long hanging sleeves which are dagged. The doublet is round necked and collarless with a short skirt. The hair is shoulder length

Caption to illustration on title page
Bonnet trimmed with ostrich feather tips. The slashed doublet reveals puffs. The full skirt is encircled with a girdle and hanger that held a dagger. The hanging sleeves of the gown reveal the decorated doublet sleeves. The squared shoes also have a slashed design, *c* 1539

Introduction

Clothing reflects the spirit of the times but fashions have always combined dignity with coquetry in greater or lesser degrees. Sometimes coquetry was to the fore, as in the case of the short tunics worn in the fifteenth century, whereas in the Tudor period, for example, robes were long and dignified. In the fourteenth century short tunics were worn over long gowns and, in more recent times, evening dress with elegant, formal tail coats, was often worn with white waistcoats and decorative, pleated shirt fronts. The narrow waist, one of the oldest forms of vanity, was prominent in Elizabethan England when men often wore tight corsets, and their doublets were lavishly padded with bombast above and below the waist. Even in the nineteenth century men wore corsets in order to improve their figures.

Dignity is also achieved by adding height to the wearer; the tall bearskins worn by Regiments of Guards, and top hats, now only worn on formal occasions, such as weddings and funerals, are examples of this. Long gowns were sometimes so extravagant, especially for Court occasions, that they too demanded respect.

The architecture of any particular period was reflected in the style of clothes worn at that time. The rounded Norman arches reflected the domed headdresses worn by the soldiers of that period. The Plantagenet influence inspired tall and perpendicular buildings; this same influence gave rise to elegant, long, trailing sleeves and close fitting tights revealing long legs.

One important aspect of men's fashion is the degree to which styles common to women's costume have been adopted. The cote-hardie, for example, was worn by both men and women, and the tall hats, decorated with ribbons and feathers, so popular in Elizabethan times, were also worn by men as much as by women. In the seventeenth century the large wigs worn by men suggested long feminine hairstyles. In the Restoration period both men and women used fans and muffs. High-heeled shoes too were favoured by both sexes. Jewellery and make-up, as well as frilled decorations, were also very popular amongst men.

Fashion was frequently set by military styles. Slashing originated in the fifteenth century when the victorious Swiss army made their underwear out of the tattered banners of their foes; this protruded through the holes of their own ragged clothing. The Steinkirk cravat originated from the Battle of this name in 1692 when the soldiers, taken by surprise, had no time to knot their cravats but simply tied them loosely, leaving the ends to be tucked in. The Duke of Wellington popularised rubber top boots, and Blucher, heavy boots. Similarly, the Earl of Cardigan gave his name to the knitted woollen jacket worn by his troops during the Crimean War.

The English dandies, or Macaronis as they were known, founded in 1764 the London Macaroni Club which reached the height of its popularity in 1772. These young gentlemen had made the Grand Tour of Italy and had a passion for all things Italian. They preferred a style of dress with a pouter-pigeon bosom and high collar and cravat with skimpy white breeches. Their wigs were extremely high and upon them they perched tiny hats. Shoes were high heeled, and the stockings striped.

In the early nineteenth century when Greek costume dress was so popular for women, men also adopted a Classical appearance. Their pantaloons were usually white or at least a light colour, and were dampened so that they fitted skin-tight. They were worn very high with the jacket cut so that the line of the legs was accentuated and elongated.

By the mid-nineteenth century London was established as the centre for men's wear. Dark lounge suits were becoming standard attire,, expressing prim and proper Victorian values and this remained unchanged for almost a century. As social standards relaxed after the First World War with the growing influence of mass manufacture, ready-to-wear garments, as well as greater interest in sports, casuals began to make an impact on general fashions. Formal clothes, such as frock and morning coats, were less commonly seen. The casual look is best illustrated by one of the most extreme modes – Oxford bags whose width, in 1925, exceeded 60 cm. Fair Isle design knitwear replaced waistcoats, Trilby and soft hats ousted top hats and shoes became more casual as fringed brogues were adopted.

Fashion was becoming available to the masses and was not just for the wealthy.

Loose Brandenburg coat with wide cuffed sleeves. The kneelength waistcoat has a row of buttons and pockets at the base. The cocked hat is decorated with ribbon loops and feathers, *c* 1674

Ancient Greek dress

Cloak or *himation* worn over a chiton and fastened with a fibula leaving the right arm free

The hair of medium length and curly, worn with a beard. The himation, elaborately draped, leaves one arm free

The most striking feature of Greek costume is the draped style which is clearly depicted on numerous statues and vases.

A linen tunic known as a *chiton*, usually long and pleated, was braided at the neck and seams. Over the chiton many men wore a cloak or *himation* with the right end flung over the left shoulder, covering the arm leaving the right arm and shoulder free.

In the fifth century BC the chitons were made from rectangular pieces of material joined together at the shoulders with pins or *fibulae*. They were belted just below the chest, with the girdle crossing over the back, then at the front and over the shoulders – catching the chiton to form sleeves, and then fastening at the back. The sides of the chiton were closed. Later these tunics had two belts, one at the waist and the other round the hips. Later sleeved tunics were introduced and these were made with larger rectangles hanging over the arms to the elbows and pinned together. There were two types of tunic, the Dorian and the Ionian – the *Dorian chiton* was sleeveless and of wool, whilst the *Ionian tunic* was generally of linen and more elegant, being long and pleated with the extra material pulled up over the belt and bloused. Sleeves could be pinned or sewn on to the tunic.

Hairstyles

Before the Persian Wars *c* 480 BC hair was worn fairly long and curled, later it became close cut. Until the fifth century BC beards were usual, but later it was mainly the older men who had beards and these were worn full and slightly pointed. Younger men were generally clean shaven. Hats were seldom worn except in extremities of weather. A conical hat, the pilos, with a narrow brim and a small peak was worn for protection against the sun; the low crowned and wide brimmed *petasos* was adopted for travelling. This hung at the back and was fastened beneath the chin, and tied front or back.

A *petasos* , low crowned and wide brimmed worn as protection against the sun

Footwear

Greeks usually went barefoot, shoes and sandals being worn only for protection and on special occasions. Sandals were fastened with straps in various ways. The soles of many shoes were studded with nails. A type of leather boot called *buskins*, usually had elevated soles to add height. They were made to fit either foot.

Accessories

Many men wore a ring with carved stones set in gold, used mainly to impress the wax on seals. Some of the wealthy young men also wore anklets.

In Ancient Greece lead oxide, chalk, and black, blue and vermilion paint were used as cosmetics as much by men as by women.

Ancient Roman dress

Sandal with a strap between the big toe and first toe, to hold it on

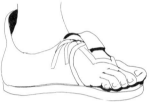

Roman sandal

Sandal with a tongue over the fastening

Roman hairstyles and beards

Roman style trousers. the sandals are laced across the foot

8

Voluminous draped toga forming
sleeves. The breeches are knee
length and tight fitting, and the
boots tied with thongs. The hair is
brushed forward

The toga is in many folds forming a
pocket or sinus in front. The sandals
are fastened with cords over the
instep. The short curly hair and
beard are in the style of the Emperor
Hadrian

Ancient Roman dress

The *toga* was the national Roman dress and was worn throughout the years of the Roman Empire. Togas were voluminous and draped around the body in folds, forming a short sleeve on the right arm which remained uncovered, but covering the left arm to the wrist. The folding was such that a pocket, called a *sinus*, was formed on the chest. The folds at the back were full enough to be able to cover the head when necessary. Tunics, copied from the Greek chiton, were worn as undergarments by the upper classes. These tunics reached halfway down the thighs, and were pulled in at the waist by a belt. Soldiers and the poorer people wore these as their sole garment. Tunics without sleeves were known as *dalmatica*.

Both togas and tunics were generally made of wool, they were decorated and had edging which indicated the wearer's profession. Togas were gradually superseded by a Grecian style mantle which was less cumbersome and fastened on the right shoulder with a clasp or ornamental brooch.

Headwear and hairstyles

Originally hair was worn long, generally brushed forward, but the shorter styles soon became more popular. One of the many styles was a circular cut with the hair turned under all round. Men usually wore no headdresses, covering their heads, when necessary, with the folds at the back of the toga. Many of the mantles had attached hoods that could be thrown back on the shoulders. Caps, known as *pileus*, were worn. Such a cap was without a brim and was made of wool. Wide brimmed hats and phrygian bonnets were also in vogue; the *phrygian bonnet* being a small close fitting woollen cap with a pointed crown which hung forward.

Footwear and legwear

There was little difference between Greek and Roman footwear. A low cut leather soled shoe, the *calceus*, was fastened with thonging. Sandals were very popular and were worn in the house, the soles fastened with cords over the instep. Other styles included straps passing through eyelets and fastening in various ways.

Breeches and trousers only began to be worn when the Romans invaded countries colder than their own. These were at first short and tight fitting, but later became longer to the ankles, and looser. The legs or thighs being wrapped with cloth for extra warmth.

Ancient and Roman Britain

Under the Roman occupation the Britons gradually discarded their fur skin coverings and *braccae*, which were a form of trousers held up at the waist with a drawstring, in favour of short tunics adapted from Roman styles. These were made of cloth woven in stripes or checks – in fact the origin of the Scottish plaids. They wore strong leather belts with swords and daggers attached. Also Roman style capes and cloaks, fastened at the right shoulder, replaced the earlier costume.

Headwear and hairstyles
Roman soldiers were clean shaven. When they invaded Britain they were astonished to find that the natives wore long drooping moustaches dyed green and blue. The typical hairstyles of the Ancient Britons were loose and flowing with locks falling over the forehead. Very little headwear was seen; occasionaly phrygian caps, or capes being pulled over the head when required.

Footwear
Footwear was a very primitive form of sandal, called crepeda, made of pieces of untanned fur-lined leather held on the foot with thonging.

Accessories
Men used pins or brooches for fastening garments. Breast-plates or *gorgets* with embossed designs were popular.

Short sleeved Norman tunic with a long sleeved linen shirt beneath. Attached to the belt is a pouch. The braes were tied with cross bands from knee to ankle. The low shoes are of leather

Loose fitting tunic with short sleeves, and shoes close fitting to the ankles

The Phrygian cap is worn. The mantle is fastened on the right shoulder with a clasp. The edges of the tunic have decorated bands of embroidery. The braes are tied and bound from the ankles to the knees ▷

Saxons and Normans

The development of dress in the post Roman period remained very simple. Linen garments were worn by the wealthy whilst the lower classes had to be content with wool. The short tunics had a large neck opening and were slit at the sides to allow for movement. The edges were decorated with embroidered bands. The narrow girdles around the waist supported a pouch wallet and, in the case of the nobility, swords and daggers. Linen shorts were sometimes worn beneath the tunics next to the skin. For ceremonial occasions the garments were ankle length with an overtunic or *roc* which was only knee length and without sleeves.

In the eleventh century tunics remained basically the same but were closer fitting to the body although a little fuller at the skirt. A *supertunic*, worn over another tunic was often made in a circular shape, loose fitting and slightly shorter than the tunic beneath. Sleeves were tight fitting or bell shaped with a wide turned back cuff.

Cloaks and *mantles* were often embroidered and fastened on the right with a clasp or brooch. They were usually square or rectangular and varied in length. Large circular capes had a hole in the centre for the head and were caught at the sides and allowed to fall in folds.

By the tenth century the rectangular mantles were worn wrapped around the body from the waist, falling in folds with the free end flung over the shoulder. Loose *braes* or breeches were worn. The ankle length braes were usually tied at the ankles and bound to the thighs. Leg bandages often replaced stockings. These were bound around the lower legs, similar to puttees. By this time close-fitting breeches and woollen tights had become popular.

After the Norman Conquest in 1066, *braes*, although not altering very much, often had attached feet with loops under the instep to hold them down. Stockings were also worn, both these and the braes being cut on the cross, and made of wool or linen. Stockings were only knee high and had embroidered tops.

The long undertunic is decorated at the hem, whilst the loose over- or supertunic has a decorated neck and sleeve edge. The sleeves are loose, bell-shaped, slightly shorter than those of the tunic beneath

Footwear
Shoes were of simple shapes made of leather, canvas or felt, low cut, and with soles usually of leather. They were close fitting around the ankles, with slits either at the sides or centre and fastened with leather thonging. Sandals were also popular, and short or mid-calf boots were not uncommon. They remained similar through the eleventh century, becoming slightly pointed, but still without heels.

11

Headwear and hairstyles

Hair was worn fairly short in the ninth and tenth centuries. It was usually combed from the crown and brushed back from the forehead.

Norman soldiers not only shaved their faces but also the backs of their heads. This style, however, soon lost its popularity and the Normans followed the British styles. After the Norman Conquest in 1066, shaving became compulsory in England, but by the fourteenth century beards, often forked, became popular, especially among the upper classes.

It was more fashionable to be bare headed, but if headwear was worn the phrygian bonnet was the mode.

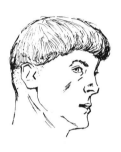

Anglo-Saxon with a long tunic over which is worn a large loose fitting cloak, slightly shorter than the tunic. The low cut shoes are plain with openings at the sides

Short hairstyle and clean shaven face. Norman

Saxon hairstyle with a forked beard and moustache

Norman hairstyle with hair at the back shaven off

Phrygian cap of the Saxon period

Leggings with cross gartered leather strips

Norman and Saxon footwear

Mediaeval

twelfth to fifteenth centuries

Cloak fastened with a brooch on the right shoulder and a phrygian cap. The hair was fairly long and curled under

The sleeveless tabard is held together at the waist with a belt. It has a large neck opening. The shoes are decorated with a cross

By the twelfth century, although still basically the same, tunics were close fitting with the skirts shorter and slit to the thighs. The sleeves were wide at the armholes, but tight fitting at the wrists. Supertunics remained unchanged, but were fur lined for warmth in cold weather.

By the thirteenth century a tunic, or *cote* as it became known, had wide armholes from shoulder to waist, the sleeves tapering to the wrists. The supertunic or *surcote* became less popular, a tabard style becoming more fashionable. Tabards were without sleeves and reached the calves; they were open at the sides being fastened only at the waist with clasps. The neck apperture was large enough to allow the head to pass through. The *garde-corps* or *herygoud* was another style of surcote, sometimes having an attached hood which fell in loose folds around the body to below the knees. The sleeves were wide and tubular, gathered at the shoulders. As the sleeves reached over the hands, vertical slits were made for the arms to be passed through. By the middle of the century pockets made their first appearance.

The fourteenth century saw the beginning of more shapely and better cut clothes, the styles of the tunics becoming shorter, revealing the legwear. Only the lower classes still wore the old styles.

Around 1335 a *doublet* or *gipon* replaced the tunic. This was worn over a shirt, and was made close fitting, shaped to the waist and padded, reaching the thighs. Fastening was either with buttons, lacing or hooks and eyes. The neckline was low and round without a collar until about 1420. The sleeves, close fitting to the wrists, closed with buttons from elbow to wrist. Later the sleeves were extended to the knuckles. Belts were not often worn and only when the cote, evolving in the fourteenth century into the *cote-hardie* was discarded was a girdle seen.

In the latter part of the fourteenth century doublets had eyelet holes around the hem to allow ties or points to be threaded and attached to matching holes on the hose.

By the second half of the fifteenth century the padded and waisted doublets became so short that they barely covered the hips, and by the end of the century, about 1485, were just waist level without the skirt part, which was optional. They fastened down the centre front with either lacing, hooks and eyes or buttons. After 1420 collars were added. These varied in style from stand-up with a V shaped front to points under the chin. Sleeves

Farm hand with his tunic hitched up over his belt. The braes are tied with a crossed band. The low crowned straw hat is held on with a string tied under the chin, *c* 1270

fitting close to the wrist were extended slightly over the hands and buttoned to the elbows. Between 1450 and 1490 high stand-up collars with wide V shaped openings gradually became so broad that the chemise or shirt beneath was visible. They were often detachable being tied at the armhole. Slashing became popular from about 1480 to the end of the century. This allowed the shirt sleeves to be pulled through.

The cote-hardie was worn as an overgarment covering the doublet. The neckline of the cote-hardie was low. The skirt, knee length and full, was left open. The elbow length sleeves had hanging cuffs that became long and narrow reaching to below the knees. These sleeves were known as *tippets*. By the latter part of the fourteenth century the cote-hardie was fastened down the front to the hem. In the early part it was shorter, reaching the knees again later. Stand-up collars were usual from around 1380-1420 after which date the cote-hardie was collarless.

The *jackets* and *jerkins* which eventually replaced the cote-hardie about 1450 had side vents and reached mid thigh. They followed the doublet styles, close fitting and waisted with flared skirts. Wide shouldered effects were achieved with shoulder pads, the sleeves gathered to the shoulder seam.

From about 1480 a V-shaped opening to the waist revealed the doublet, or sometimes a stomacher was inserted. The sleeves, narrowing to the wrists were full, often slashed and laced, revealing an undersleeve. They could also be turned back to the elbow, the contrasting lining giving a deep cuff effect. Long hanging sleeves to the knees were also seen. These were sometimes joined at the back to keep them out of the way, with slits for the arms to protrude.

The *houppelande* was introduced towards 1380, remaining popular under that name until about 1450, when it became known just as a gown. This was put on over the head, often made with a high standing collar until the fifteenth century when they were mainly without collars, a V-shaped front being popular around 1430 to 1480. U shapes were also popular from about 1450 to 1470 but Rounded necklines remained fashionable throughout the century. Flat square-cut collars with wide lapels, sometimes fur trimmed, became popular from around 1485 to 1540. The folds which eminated from the shoulders were held in place at the waist by a girdle and side seams were left open for a short length from the hem.

Hanging sleeves were fashionable throughout and had an opening in the front of the upper arm for the sleeved doublet to protrude. Sleeves were often dagged.

Outdoor wear

Cloaks and *mantles* with hoods attached, remained fashionable only until about 1430 from which time they were only worn for extra warmth or for travelling. They were full and were fastened either with a clasp or cord. Another popular way was for one corner to be pulled through a ring sewn to the other and tied in a knot. Long circular cloaks were lavishly lined when worn by the wealthier classes. Shoulder capes were also popular. They generally had low collars and were knee length, fastening down the front with a close row of buttons. Thigh length capes, sometimes with hoods, could also be worn. Shoulder capes with dagged edges retained their popularity for 100 years from about 1330.

Fourteenth-century dagged hat

The short doublet barely covered the hips. It is fastened down the front with lacing. The long sleeves are slashed to allow the shirt sleeves beneath to protrude. The long overgown has slit hanging sleeves, fur trimmed, c 1483

Over the long undertunic is worn a shorter overtunic with wide sleeves. The shoes, close to the ankles, are slit either side

The short doublet attached to the hose with points threaded through matching eyelet holes. The soft leather boots were plain and just pulled on, early fourteenth century

The gipon is padded and has bagpipe sleeves. Around the waist the belt holds a sword and dagger

The hat had a turned-up dagged brim and the short cape is also dagged. the gipon is thigh length with a belt. The thick loose overstockings were turned down just below the knees, late fourteenth century

The jerkin ending just above the knees has full sleeves to the wrists. The gown, slightly longer, has a broad fur collar, and the slit hanging sleeves are also fur edged, c 1483

The low crowned hat has a turn-up brim and the collarless cote-hardie has dagged hanging sleeves. the gipon or doublet beneath has a stand-up collar and long tight sleeves, fourteenth century

The houppelande has the side seams open revealing the hose and calf length boots, the hair is in a bowl shaped fashion and turned under all round, c 1422

Thigh length houppelande with a high standing collar fastened with buttons. The deep folds of the garment are held in place with a waist girdle. The closed hanging sleeves fall in wide folds to a wristband. The long hose are soled, c 1399

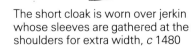

The short cloak is worn over jerkin whose sleeves are gathered at the shoulders for extra width, c 1480

The long hose are held up to the knees with cross garters. The short jerkin is closed with lacing

The dagged edged hood and cape are worn over the short cote-hardie with the hanging streamers, c 1366

Underwear

A garment worn over a shirt and beneath the doublet, the *petticote*, was worn from about 1450 to 1515, and was short and well padded, close fitting with or without sleeves. The neck was usually rounded as the garment was generally worn for extra warmth.

Legwear

Breeches and braes became shorter and were later worn only as undergarments. Long hose were worn with a strap under the foot, or something – following an earlier Saxon fashion – the footwear was attached. These usually had thin leather soles. Stockings had ornamental borders. They had a protruding piece in the front that could be pulled over the braes and attached to the girdle with ties. Stockings were often decorated in contrasting colours, parti-coloured or vertically striped hose also became fashionable and were worn until the early part of the fifteenth century.

Garters were tied just beneath the knees with the ends of the material either tucked in or left hanging. Soled hose were also worn with the feet shaped to the foot. When, in the late fourteenth century, long pointed toes became the mode, they were often stuffed to exaggerated length.

In the fifteenth century separate stockings were still attached to the doublets with ties or points through matching eyelet holes. Joined hose, similar to present-day tights, were beginning to be worn with the shorter cut clothes. At first they only reached the hips, but later in the century, about 1475, they went as high as the waist. The seat part, also known as breeches, was often of a different colour and material from the legs.

From the fifteenth century breeches were held up by points or tagged laces. These were slotted through eyelet holes in both the breeches and the upper garments or *pourpoint* as it was called at first. Striped or parti-coloured hose again became fashionable in about 1485. The method of fastening to the doublet or petticote remained the same. When the hose became too tight for movement a gusset was inserted to ease the strain. This was the origin of the *codpiece* which was a small bag with a flap at the fork of the hose, closed by ties. It was also known as a *braguette* (from the French) and was popular in the fourteenth and fifteenth centuries when it was rendered more prominent with padding.

Footwear

In the earlier mediaeval period the wealthier classes wore more elegant low cut shoes, the styles becoming more pointed than previously. This style was adopted from the Orient and brought over by the Crusaders. Shoes were made to fit either foot which, with wear, shaped themselves. Those that fitted around the ankles were usually laced at the side. Piked or pointed shoes became very popular around 1360, although they were at first banned under a Sumptuary law by Edward III (1327-1377). Embroidery and punched patterns were fashionable. These pointed or piked shoes were introduced into England during the Norman Conquest. Throughout the Mediaeval period they became more pointed until,

Pointed shoe with a punched-out pattern, *c* 1360

Thirteenth-century pointed shoe

Long piked shoe with the pointed toe attached with a chain and tassels to the front, fourteenth century

Long-toed wooden pattern worn over a decorated shoe, fourteenth century

Rose window style shoe

eventually, the toes were so long that they had to be chained up and fastened at the knees.

The long pointed toes went out of fashion in the 1410s becoming round toed until about 1460, when the long piked points again became the mode.

Thick loose *overstockings* shaped to the feet, were worn turned down to the knees.

Ankle hugging shoes and boots were worn mainly by the poor, although it became fashionable to wear calf length boots with the uppers turned down to reveal coloured linings. A loose fitting *boot* or *buskin* reached just below the calf, otherwise there was very little change until the fourteenth century.

Riding boots, shaped to the thighs were fastened with buttons, lacing or buckles just below the calf, but by about 1395 a new type of fastening with hooks on the outer side was introduced. Other styles were still loose and shapeless. Short or calf length buskins were worn throughout the fifteenth century, fastened by lacing, hooks and eyes or buckles. Thigh length buskins fastened at the sides often had the tops turned down to give a deep cuff. Special socks were generally worn over the hose to protect them when buskins were worn.

Galoshes and *clogs*, as well as wooden pattens attached to shoes with leather straps were also worn.

Spurs, even worn with soled hose were fashionable for civilians as well as the military.

Coif tied under the chin, worn beneath a liripipe, *c* 1320

Floppy hat with crown pulled forward over the rolled brim, *c* 1410

Long pointed shoe with strap fastening

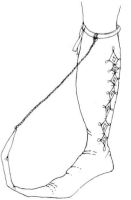

Shoe ornamentation up the sides, the beginning of clocks. The long pointed toe was attached with a chain to just below the knee

Cowl hood

Tall hat with a rolled brim, *c* 1412

The extended piece of the liripipe could be of any length, fourteenth century

Headwear and hairstyles

During the Plantagagenet period from 1154, headwear gradually began to alter. The phrygian caps lost their popularity after about two centuries, and cowls or hoods with short attached capes became the mode. Also seen were stalked caps, decorated at the top point with stems or stalks or occasionally a knob. Sometimes they were also seen with a narrow rolled brim. Low crowned hats with large brims were often worn over hoods.

Coifs or close-fitting linen bonnets covered the hair and ears, and were tied with strings under the chin. These could be worn alone or beneath other headwear. These styles remained popular throughout the thirteenth century.

Stalked berets, especially for country wear continued to be popular in the fourteenth century, as were wide brimmed hats, with the brim turned up at the back, and the front shaped into a long peak. Coifs also remained popular throughout the century. Skull caps were also worn beneath headwear. As the century progressed more ornamentation and trimmings were seen. Dyed feathers and plumes were fastened to the headwear with jewelled ornaments. Decorative headbands also became the mode.

In the fifteenth century hats varied greatly in styles. Amongst the popular fashions in the early 1400s tall hats with wide rolled brims were being worn. Floppy bag shaped hats were fashionable in the 1430s as well as Robin Hood styles with a tapering crown and a peaked brim turned up at the back. Simple straw hats, flat pork-pie bonnets with turned up brims were popular from about 1475.

In the fourteenth century hoods developed an extended hanging tail piece called a *liripipe* which could be left hanging or twisted around the head in the style of a turban. Towards the latter part of the century the hood-turban altered with the face opening made to fit better.

Hoods became unfashionable about 1450, although with the liripipe they remained popular until around 1480. The hood-turban became known as a *chaperon* and consisted of a padded roll, a cape part or gorget, and liripipe or hanging piece.

Shoulder length hair parted on either side with the front in a fringe again became popular in the twelfth century. Beards and moustaches were also seen. Beards were often forked and covered in ointments to stiffen them. At night special bags covered them for protection. Both beards and moustaches became shorter towards the middle of the twelfth century when hair reached the nape of the neck. Forelocks and fringes were worn.

In the fourteenth century hairstyles changed very little, hair being worn in varying lengths. In the 1350s it was brushed forward with the sides and back rolled over. It was more fashionable to be clean shaven, although if beards were worn, they were generally forked. Towards the end of the century both hair and beards became longer again.

Bowl shaped hairstyles remained in fashion until about 1460 with the hair brushed from the crown and turned under all round. Beards and moustaches were seldom seen with the shorter hair.

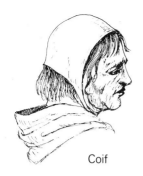

Coif

Baldrick and belt profusely decorated with bells, c 1450

Purse with three tassels attached to a girdle, c 1490

A modified bowl crop with longer hair covering the forehead, ears and nape of the neck remained popular until about 1475. A similar style – the long pageboy cut became the mode from about 1465; the fringe could be curled under. These styles were kept in place with the aid of resins and egg whites. Blond hair was fashionable, saffron and onion skins being used as dyes.

Accessories

From as early as the Saxon period *pouch wallets* were worn either at the belt or slung from a shoulder belt. By the thirteenth century girdles and belts were highly decorated and tied like a sash. The ornamental girdles were tied in front with the ends left hanging. Pouches or purses were attached by two straps. *Daggers* were also suspended from a cord attached to the girdle and back of the pouch.

By the fifteenth century ornamental girdles were made of jointed metal clasps and were worn mainly by the nobility. They often had decorative bells attached as well as the usual pouches, detachable pockets, keys and daggers. Around 1400 there was a craze for sewing bells onto clothes. These were generally sewn along the borders of the gipon, and on garters and shoes. Although this was essentially a male fashion there is a mention in the famous nursery rhyme of the 'fine Lady at Banbury Cross with rings on her fingers and bells on her toes'. It was from this fashion that the jester's cap with bells can be dated. Purses with three tassels were also very popular. *Shoulder belts* and *baldricks* were also heavily decorated with bells and jewellery.

Gloves, originally a continental fashion were first only worn by the nobility in mediaeval times. By the twelfth century they were richly embroidered and inlaid with jewels for the wealthier. Glove makers were recorded as early as 1295. Gloves became universal wear in the fourteenth century the gauntlet cuffs embroidered for the upper classes whilst the others wore types of mittens with thumb and first finger separate.

Dagging around the edges of the tunics or supertunics was first seen in Plantagenet times. This was in the form of vandyking with deep indentations.

Swiss soldiers made their undergarments from the tattered banners of their defeated enemies and pulled these through the *slashings* of the battle dress. This fashion rapidly spread throughout Europe, and at its height even shoes, hats and gloves as well as doublet and hose were slashed to allow for the under fabric to protrude.

Walking sticks were often carried.

From around the middle of the fourteenth century black became the accepted colour for mourning.

Sixteenth century

The padded doublet has rolled wings on the shoulder seams from which eminate full sleeves. The neck and wrist ruffs match. The shirt beneath the doublet is pulled through the slashes in bunches at the waist, and the breeches also have slashings. Garters are worn just below the knees and the shoes have slashed designs. the hat, like an inverted flowerpot has the brim curled up and bound. c 1578

The doublet and trunk hose are bombasted, the hose also being slashed, and the doublet in the peascod style. The short cape has a small collar, c 1590

In the early Tudor times of Henry VIII (1485-1509) the change from the mediaeval fashions was slow. It was when dress became shorter that more extravagant styles emerged.

The *doublet* remained close fitting. From 1485 it could be skirted to the hips, but more often it only reached the waist, without skirts. By 1530 skirts were again attached. When full, they fell over the hips, but the shorter skirts were often looped, tabbed or scalloped, tabs being sewn to the waistline which could be braided or embroidered. These decorative additions were also known as *pickadils*. Tabs or pickadils could be overlapped or sewn edge to edge. The skirts varied as fashions changed. In the latter part of the century they became very short and almost hidden by the waist girdles. They were also sometimes flared, hiding the points that joined the hose to the doublet.

Eyelet holes around the waist of the doublets matched similar holes around the hose through which points were threaded and tied in bows. These points were usually hidden beneath the doublet or its skirts. The points, especially for the wealthier could be tipped with decorative metal tags. A small knotted sash or girdle around the waist was also popular.

Doublets were often padded just above the waistline. This was known as bombast, and by 1577 bombasting was very fashionable. Buckram or pasteboard in the front was also used as stiffening.

In the second part of the century doublet fronts became more pointed as the waistline curved downwards. From about 1575 a Dutch fashion – the peascod belly – became fashionable. Even more padding or bombast was required from the waist in order to produce an over-hanging projection. The buttons fastened down the centre front which protruded slightly from the chest to give the peascod effect.

In the early part of the sixteenth century the doublets were mainly without collars and the fairly low V-front opening was covered with either a shirt or *stomacher*, also known as a *partlet* or *plackard*. These inserts were generally of brocade and matched the detachable sleeves. From about 1530 the necklines became rounder. In the later part of the century standing collars became the mode, the front falling away to allow ruffs to be tilted forward. The larger ruffs were supported by stiff *tabs* known also as *pickadils*.

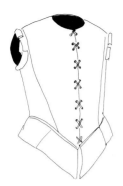

Sleeveless buff leather jerkin fastened with lacing down the front, *c* 1580

Sleeveless jerkin, the wings concealing the shoulder welts. There are points at the waist which are tabbed. The ruff is goffered. The tall hat has a small hatband with a feather trimming, *c* 1580

Mandilion fashionable from the 1570s to the 1620s, could be worn sideways, one sleeve hanging in the front

The fashionable man of the 1570s wore slightly padded doublets with full sleeves and rolled wings on the shoulders. The basques or skirts were long and full. It was quite usual for sleeves to be made detachable and to be full at the shoulders tapering to a close fitting wrist. The fullness of the sleeves was paned or slashed revealing the shirt or contrasting lining. It was also fashionable, towards the end of the century for the doublet sleeves to just hang loose, as a sham sleeve. Sometimes it was even seen to have two sleeves, one sham and one functional. Detachable sleeves were concealed at the joins or points with wings. These shoulder welts were in varying shapes. They could be crescent shaped, scalloped, tabbed or even in loops. Rolls were also sometimes placed over the armholes. Sleeves did not alter a great deal throughout the period, generally being padded and close fitting to the wrists. Vertical slits that were closed with a row of buttons were sometimes also used as pockets to store personal belongings. Distended sleeves were stiffened with wire or bone. These were known as *farthingale* sleeves. They became popular in the Elizabethan period *c* 1580.

Jackets or *jerkins* were seldom padded, but they could be lined. They were worn over doublets, were high waisted and close fitting. The skirts always covered the doublets whatever the fashionable length. The skirts were hip length or longer when jerkins were worn for riding. The deep V-shaped opening in the front showed either the doublet itself or a plackard which is a stomacher or chestpiece covering the opening.

In the early years a narrow rever from waist to shoulder where it widened to form a rounded flat collar, gradually changed to a more square form around 1540, when a narrow stand-up collar was attached. As collars increased in size on the doublets, the jacket collars did likewise. Fastening was similar to the doublets – buttons, lacing or hooks and eyes – to the waist, although often the front was left open. Sleeves were usually short and puffed to the elbows, but longer sleeves were close fitting from elbow to wrist. Slashings and ribbon-like strips called *panes*, were similar to those of the doublets.

Jerkins were often seen with just sham hanging sleeves. Sleeveless jerkins were also fashionable and were made to fit over doublets with armholes and waist decorated with pickadils. From the mid 1500s long sham hanging sleeves, like streamers without armholes were merely ornamentation. It was also the mode to wear hanging sleeves, one worn and the other just left hanging. Also in the second part of the century, buff jerkins, originally worn by the military, were of leather. The body of these jerkins was in narrow panes with a plain collar and yoke. These were generally sleeveless with just *wings* which were stiffened and decorated bands, often crescent shaped, projecting over the shoulder seams. The short skirts were either tabbed in pickadils or paned.

A short waist-length, coat like garment, a *petticote*, was worn between doublet and shirt. The neckline was low and rounded. If sleeves were present they were usually detachable. As petticotes were worn mainly for warmth they were generally padded. Hose could be attached to the petticotes as they were to the doublets, with eyelet holes and lacing. Later, the petticote became known as a waistcoat, and was fashionable in this style until about 1625.

The doublet has a rounded neckline and slashed sleeves. The front of the gown is fur trimmed. A flat cap with feathers is worn, c 1530

Close cut hair. The hat is a flat velvet bonnet with a very shallow brim ornamented with pearls and beads on a narrow hatband. On the left is a drooped feather held on with an ornament

Halo bonnet trimmed with ostrich feathers, c 1537

Gowns were worn over doublets. These were made very broad across the shoulders and hung loosely down in folds, mainly left open in the front, often with a girdle around the waist. The front edges were turned back to form revers to give a wide collar at the back as they broadened at the shoulders. If the revers remained narrow, a small roll collar was achieved. The gown varied in length from short to knee length and was popular for horse riding. Ankle length gowns were worn for ceremonial occasions. The sleeves varied according to the prevailing fashions. From about 1530 large puffs at the shoulders helped give the impression of broadness, and hanging sleeves could be attached. Before this, full, turned-back cuffs were popular with a narrow sleeve. The arms often protruded from slits in the hanging sleeves. Gowns were generally made of damasks or velvets, fur or velvet trimmed and lined in silks.

Outdoor wear

From about 1545 cloaks were often worn instead of gowns. They were usually semi-circular with a collar attached. They were generally fastened by a cord over one shoulder. A short shoulder cape known as a *tippet* was often worn over cloaks or capes throughout the century. The wealthier classes wore different cloaks for special occasions. For instance cloaks worn for riding were often slit at the sides or back. The length also varied from mid-thigh to the ankles by the latter part of the century.

Collars and necklines also varied. Turned down or standing collars attached to the lapels which continued down to the hem were not unusual. The standing collars could be full or standing only at the back. Collarless cloaks were also seen and in that case the edge of the cloaks had a trimmed border.

Cloaks with the sleeves either plain or puffed, and hanging sleeves attached at the back were fashionable from mid century. These usually were no longer than thigh length and were closed with tasselled cords. Spanish type cloaks were popular for almost a century. They had attached hoods at the back which were wide, pointed and decorated with loops and buttons, but purely ornamental. At the start of the sixteenth century they were hip length, and by the middle only reached the waist with a narrow turned down collar and lapel. This type of cape could be worn over one or both shoulders.

A long French type of cloak, cut circular, fell at least to knee length. The collar was very wide at the shoulders reaching to the elbows and could be draped back. This was known as a *manteau à la rietre*.

The Dutch cloak, full and waist length, had very wide sleeves with lavish bands to conceal the seams.

At this period a broad appearance was very fashionable.

Towards the middle of the century a short loose coat, open at the sides, a cross between a cloak and a jerkin, known as a *mandilion*, was also popular. It had a short standing collar, was fastened from neck to chest, and put on over the head. The sleeves were of the hanging type, and later became sham. The mandilion was generally worn either over the shoulders with the sleeves left to hang at the sides or with the sleeves hanging front and back with the panels covering the shoulders.

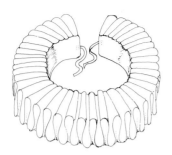

Cartwheel goffered ruff with cord for tying

Supportasse made of wire worn around the neck to support the large ruffs. It was also known as a *rebato*

The uppers have three long cuttes and a series of small ones around the heel. Across the instep are three rows of ornamental loops. This type of shoe usually matched the hose either in colour or material, *c* 1537

Chopine all in one with the shoe, *c* 1547

Cassocks, about hip length, worn mainly by the middle classes were wide loose coats. The collars were narrow and standing, and the sleeves close fitting either wrist or elbow length.

Long loose overcoats, known as *gabardines* had wide sleeves. They were worn either with or without belts, and mainly by horsemen.

Neckwear

In the earlier part of the century the neckbands of shirts were decorated with lace edging which later developed into a frill, until it became a small ruff in the Elizabethan era. This followed the mode of a turned down collar, falling band or pleated and goffered collar. These collars increased gradually in width and lay flat over the shoulders. The goffered ruff which originated from a frilled neckband became fashionable in the 1560s. Larger ruffs only became possible when in 1573 heated poking sticks in steel were produced instead of the old method of using wooden or bone sticks. Starch for stiffening was introduced a little earlier in 1560.

Wrist and neck ruffs were usually matching and known as a *suit of ruffs*. Ruffs were attached beneath the chin with cords or tasselled strings, although when first worn, they were attached to the shirts. Only later in the second part of the century did they become detached. In the 1560s ruffs were quite small and closed, becoming larger in the 1570s. After 1580 the ruff became very large, the width varying from 9 in. to 15 in. (23 cm to 38 cm). The full length of the band could be as much as 8 yards (about 7.25 metres). These became known as *cartwheel ruffs*. Sometimes more starching could not always support them high at the back, so a wire support known as a *supportasse* or *rebato* was worn beneath the ruff.

Legwear and footwear

Stockings (similar to modern day tights) were made up of *netherstocks* and *upperstocks*. The netherstocks were the lower stocking part, whilst the upperstocks were the upper joined part, or, as previously known, the *breeches*. These were made of material cut on the cross and, until about 1515, slashed. Later the top portion became fuller, from which the trunk hose fashions developed. *Trunk hose* were also known as *French hose*, *slops*, *round hose*, or *trunk breeches*. Slops gradually increased in size between 1565 and 1575 with the greatest width in the middle. They were made with a narrow waistband and not with a hip yoke to which they were originally attached.

Paning was still popular with a great deal of ornamentation and embroidery. Bombast and whalebone busks were used to keep the slops puffed out. Instead of being attached to the doublet itself, they were attached to the lining with lacing.

Canions appeared around 1570. They were the upper part of hose and were also known as upperstocks. They were buckled either just above or below the knees. The lower part, or netherstocks, were secured above the knees with garters. Also fashionable in the latter part of the century were *Venetian slops* or *breeches*. These were full and wide at the top, gathered

PLATE 1 *Left* Over the long undertunic is worn a wide sleeved embroidered overtunic, Norman period, c 1087. *Centre* The turban headwear made from a liripipe, the hanging piece falls over the shoulder and is tucked into the waist belt. The tabard is fur edged. The hose are parti-coloured and the shoes fit the foot and end in long points, c 1380. *Background right* The doublet is square necked and slashed revealing the shirt beneath. The knee length jacket has short puffed sleeves. The shoes are wide and square toed with a slashed design. The halo trimmed bonnet is edged with ostrich feathers, c 1540. *Right* The doublet with a peascod body and long pointed waist has a high neckline surmounted by a small lace ruff. The trunk hose are bombasted and paned. The short flared sleeved cloak has a standing collar, c 1560

PLATE 2   Left *The full wig is made of long curls hanging over the shoulders. The hat is low crowned with a wide brim and ribbon loops. The coat is knee length and slightly waisted without a collar. The long close fitting sleeves have turn-back cuffs. The breeches are of the petticoat style, c 1678.*   Centre left *The tricorne hat is edged with braid with a button and loop, and worn over a long full bottomed wig. The collarless coat has close fitting sleeves with large cuffs. It is worn open* and reveals the hip length waistcoat. The boots are square toed worn with spur leathers, c 1715.*   Centre right *The hat is tall, crowned in beaver with a wide curling brim. The cut-away jacket with the high collar, almost to the ears, is worn with a waistlength waistcoat with revers. The breeches fasten at the knees with ties, c 1790.* Right *The jerkin is winged and has sham hanging sleeves. The fashionable cloak-bag breeches are worn with high leather cup-topped boots, c 1625*

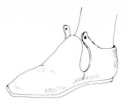

Leather shoe. The side cut low and the front curving over the instep forming a short strap with eyelet holes through which a ribbon could be threaded for tying, *c* 1558

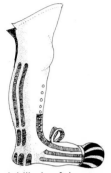

Broad duck-billed soft boots, buttoning up the front and the toes padded for extra width, early sixteenth century

The long soft leather boots fit closely to the leg. The two straps sewn inside are attached to waistbelt beneath the slops. The spurs have large loose rowels that jingled, *c* 1588

Flat woollen cap also known as a *Monmouth cap*, rather like a tam'-o'-shanter in shape

in at the waist, with hip padding, narrowing towards the knees where they were fastened with points and trimmed with lace. The codpiece continued in fashion until about 1575, becoming smaller with less bombast from about the 1540s. It was finally discarded at the end of the century, and was replaced by a vertical slit in front which was concealed in folds of material.

The hose and doublets were still joined by passing metal tipped strings through eyelet holes called *trussing the points*.

In 1589 William Lee, a graduate clergyman from Cambridge, invented a stocking frame which enabled stockings to be mechanically knitted. In 1598 it was adapted to take not only worsted, but also silk, and when the frame came into use the tailored, cut on the cross, material stockings were replaced by knitted stockings, although hand-knitted ones were already popular amongst the wealthy. With the advent of silk stockings, boot hose developed. They were very practical, although not so fashionable, being worn mainly over silk stockings as a protection when boots were worn. Stockings became ornamental with embroidery.

Garters were worn just below the knees with a bow on the outside, not just to hold the stockings in place, but also as an ornamental accessory. In the early part of the century overstockings were worn inside boots to protect the underhose; they were loose and wide at the tops so that they could be turned down to form a cuff.

Shoes which fitted close to the ankle were popular, as were low cut shoes fastened by a strap. As shoes were not always waterproof – some being made of cloth – pattens were worn in inclement weather. These gradually evolved into overshoes with wooden soles. They could have either a toepiece into which the shoes fitted or leather cross straps.

Buttons and hooks could be used as shoe fastenings with eyelet holes just punched into the leather, although the holes could be sewn around with a buttonhole stitch for the wealthier.

As shoes became broader, the toes were padded at the side making them almost as broad a they were long. Slashed designs, similar to those on clothing revealed puffs of lace or material. These shapes were known as *duckbilled* and became so broad that Henry VIII limited the width to 6 in. (15 cm). The soles of shoes followed the shape of the feet. Shoes were often of the same colour as the hose. Linen linings or stockings were worn if shoes or boots were rough inside.

For many years footwear was simple, just following the shape of the foot, with the uppers either just slashed or in cut designs. Heels were not seen in England until the middle of the sixteenth century.

Long *boots* were generally used for riding and were turned down above the knees to reveal the linings which were of a contrasting colour. From the inside two straps were attached to the slops or breeches to hold them up. For riding boots and buskins were often slit at the top of the back seam to facilitate movement. Some leather boots were tight fitting and shaped to the legs with decorative rosettes and knee slashings to reveal the silk linings. Buskins were sometimes fur lined, made of a softer leather or even velvet. Boots and high shoes could be laced front or side or buckled. The top buckles could be concealed with the folded back stockings.

(a) Tall crowned trimmed soft bonnet, c 1575. (b) Tall round crowned hat with a narrow brim, c 1570. (c) Bonnet pleated to a small brim, c 1560. (d) Soft bonnet, c 1520. (e) Flat cap with feather decoration, c 1543

Underwear

In the Elizabethan era men wore corsets, the same shape as women's with an inverted triangular front panel. Long white linen drawers were worn beneath amply cut breeches, and tied with ribbons at the waist. They were generally just knee length, but if worn long they could have attached feet, or bands that passed under the instep to hold them down.

Night attire

Nightrailes, or night garments were worn by fashionable men as well as women. They were made like a chemise, loose and with embroidery around the neck and sleeves. The small ruffs were often edged with lace.

Nightcaps were bag shaped, rounded at the top and turned up with a small brim, never altering in shape. They were also known as *biggins*. They became so ornately embroidered that elderly men also wore them in the daytime.

Headwear

The use of indoor headwear persisted. From the beginning of the century until about 1545 small bonnets were popular with a variety of brims. During the 1520s until the latter part of the century the shallow brim was turned up. The crown was usually low and flat, obscured by the decoration of plumes and feathers drooping down. The popular way of wearing this style was with a sideways tilt, often over a caul. Narrow hatbands were often ornamented with buttons, jewels, aiglettes or precious stones. sometimes the brims could be worn turned up, 'halo' style.

From the 1560s soft crowned bonnets with narrow brims were fashionable. The height of the crown varied and the bonnets worn at an angle, with feathers often used as ornamentation. From the 1580s soft crowns were stiffened with buckram. The fullness of the crown was folded or pleated into the narrow brim. Wide brimmed and low-crowned hats could be worn tilted back or slung over the back suspended from cords. The hats, popular from 1490 until the first decade of the sixteenth century, were profusely decorated with plumes and feathers. Flat hats, popular from the 1530s until the 1570s were low-crowned and plain with just a minimum of decoration, such as a single brooch or feather. From the early 1560s high-crowned conical hats became fashionable. The brim could be worn in various ways, either flat, turned up or down or even rolled like a modern bowler hat. One type was known as a *copotain*, usually made of blocked felt with a small rolled up brim. Hats with hard foundations first became fashionable around 1575. They were like inverted flower pots with a hatband and curled up brim bound with an edging.

A small round cap with a turned up brim was fashionable throughout the century. It had a flat crown and was made in four sections. The brim could be cut away at the front leaving just back and sides. Sometimes the sides were turned down over the ears or turned up and buttoned on top. Full crowns, similar to berets, pleated on to a headband, were also popular.

In the first years of Queen Elizabeth's reign flat caps became very fashionable, the crown gradually becoming fuller. These continued to be worn until at least the end of the century.

e

Hair brushed forward into locks that mingle with the beard and moustache which was stiffened with wax. The high collar is surmounted by a small neck ruff, c 1559

Gloves showing cuttes around the fingers to reveal the rings worn

These flat caps were also known as *bonnets*. A typical style of knitted wool cap, very much in vogue was a flat mushroom shape over a narrow brim. The flat cap, known as a *City flat cap* (worn a great deal by business men and called a *statute* by William Shakespeare) became an essential part of costume. An edict was made by the Sumptuary Court in 1571 and read as follows:

'if any person above six years of age (except maidens, ladies, gentlewomen, nobles, knights, gentlemen of twenty marks by year in lands, and their heirs, and such as have borne office of worship) have not worn upon the Sunday and Holyday (except it be the time of his travell out of the city, town, or hamlet, where he dwelleth) upon his head one cap of wool, knit, thicked, and dressed in England, and only dressed and finished by some of the trade of cappers, shall be fined 3s. 4d. for each day's trangression.'

However this law was difficult to enforce and was evaded and violated; it was later repealed in 1597.

A tam-o'shanter type cap known as a *Monmouth cap* (after the town where they were principally manufactured) was very popular, especially amongst seamen.

Hairstyles

Over this century hairstyles changed considerably. In the early part hair was generally shoulder length, often with a fringe. Hair became shorter in the 1520s, bobbed to chin level. From the 1560s hair cut close to the head became fashionable. It was brushed up into a bristle effect and held in place with gum. From the 1580s hairstyles became very elaborate falling again to the shoulders with curls. A lock of hair curled to hang over one shoulder down to the chest was known as a *lovelock* and was popular from the 1590s to the 1650s.

Until the 1530s the face was usually clean shaven but then a short moustache and beard became popular, this was worn in various styles, square, round or pointed with one or two points. A Spanish pointed style became popular around 1550.

Beards were worn with descriptive name such as forked, spade, whispy. The *pickdevant* was a short brushed up moustache and beard combined. The word moustache came into being in the Elisabethan era, and originally derived from the Greek 'mustax' meaning upper lip. Beards were seldom seen without accompanying moustaches. They were quite often stiffened with wax, powdered and perfumed. Curling irons were also applied to shape them, and dying in fashionable red was also popular.

Accessories

Gloves with short cuffs in contrasting colours and material were worn by the wealthier classes. Large gauntlets richly embroidered and fringed edging was also fashionable. Gloves with slashings around the fingers allowed for the large rings, so popular in Elizabethan times, to protrude. Imported perfumed gloves known as *Frangipani* took their name from the

Italian Count Frangipani, who added alcohol to solid perfume. Later in the century when gloves were manufactured in England, they became more commonplace. Mittens, like gloves were made of silks, velvets, satins or leather.

Decorative *handkerchiefs* were edged with lace and embroidery and carried in the hand, although with the advent of pockets and deep folds in the doublets, they were often out of sight. A drawstring type of purse was also carried, either attached to the girdle, or in the pocket or folds of the doublet.

Scarves, first seen in the 1580s, were not fashionable, but worn mainly for warmth.

The fashionable dandies carried *fans* and *mirrors*.

The doublet is slightly padded and the sleeves end with small wrist ruffs with a roll or padded welt at the shoulder joins. The venetian slops were not stuffed but fell loosely to the thighs with the lower part of the legs in netherstocks and ankle boots. The soft crown of the hat was pleated into the brim and masked by a silk or velvet hatband, *c* 1578

The dress was popular among ordinary people. The slightly padded doublet has a small skirt and shoulder welts, and the small neck ruff matches those of the sleeves. The full slops are paned. The netherstocks are worn over the upperstocks. The ample cloak reaches to the knees, *c* 1590

The long shoulder length hair is worn with a vandyke beard and moustache. The high waisted doublet has deep skirts and is buttoned down the front. There are also wings and a falling collar. The breeches are long and oval shaped reaching from a high waistline to just below the knees and fastened with bows. Shoe roses of ribbon loops could also be seen, c 1635

The loose coat has short sleeves ending with ribbon loops. The shirt sleeves with lace cuffs protrude. The neckcloth is of lace. The shoes with medium to high heels are decorated with a large ribbon bow, c 1664

Seventeenth century

The rich formality of Elizabethan dress which was still being worn during the reign of James I (1603-1625) gave way to the French influence. Men's attire acquired a more graceful appearance with softer materials and less bombast; garments were looser fitting.

Charles II brought back with him many French fashions from his exile after the Commonwealth period. These included petticoat breeches over which were worn loose shirts. Hairpowder and enormous periwigs were also popular. Men painted their faces, and carried muffs and fans. This was undoubtedly the period of the most effeminate dress for men in England.

Doublets

In the early part of the century doublets continued to be worn. Until about 1630 the long-waisted close-fitting styles were popular. From the late 1590s they were stiffened with whalebone, the fronts being lined with either canvas or buckram. The peascod front gradually became less fashionable. From about 1620 to 1665 a belly-piece, formed by two triangular sections of stiff material sewn together at waist level into the lining, gave a point down the centre front into the waistline.

Until about 1610 the doublet skirts flared out from the waist, the basque being formed by about eight separate tabs with slight overlaps. After that date until about 1630, the tabs were often deeper, and the two tabs centre front came to a sharp point, either edge to edge or overlapping. As the doublet waistline was raised around 1620, the tabs became longer and were slightly reduced in number. The waistline became so high around 1630 that the number of tabs was reduced to four, two in front and two behind.

Narrow swordbelts with decorated hangers were worn around the waistline until about 1625. They were suspended by ornamental shoulder belts, known as *baldricks*. Collars were high and fastened with buttons and loops, unlike the doublets themselves that were fastened with hooks and eyes, points or buttons and buttonholes.

Sleeves were generally straight and close-fitting with wings at the shoulders. These became broader, but by 1640 were out of fashion. Sleeves were fastened from wrist to elbow, the same way as the doublet fronts. A short buttoned slit in the sleeves sometimes acted as a pocket. From about 1620 to 1640 slashings revealing the full shirt beneath extended from the shoulder to the elbow. Slashing and panes were also seen in vertical slits on the chest and back of the doublets.

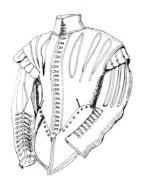

Early seventeenth century doublet

The coat worn open to the waist had large pocket openings low on the coat and revealed the waistcoat. The sleeves have deep cuffs with ornamental buttons that match those by the pocket. The cloak is three quarter length. On the full-bottomed wig is worn a low crowned, wide brimmed boater-shaped hat with a buckled hatband. The shoes are also buckled, *c* 1670

From the early 1640s doublets began to change radically. The stiff corset shape was replaced by a looser fitting style. Padding became obsolete but the belly-piece did remain in fashion for a while. The eyelets that had been used for joining doublet and hose became purely ornamental without any functional use. The tabs, instead of being pointed, were squared off. Collars remained. The sleeves were not as close fitting and were buttoned at the wrists. They could also end at the elbows with deep turned-back cuffs.

From the late 1640s until the 1670s doublets became much shorter and were only slightly padded in the front and were without linings. The skirts became so short that they were just tabbed borders. The short doublets did not reach to the breeches, which themselves sometimes only reached the hips, and the gap was filled with the voluminous protruding shirt. Sometimes the doublets were only fastened half way down the chest. By about 1670 they were replaced by coats.

Coats

After the 1660s doublets were being replaced by coats and waistcoats. Jacket, waistcoat and coat, as known nowadays, became general terms from the 1660s. The first coats that replaced doublets only fitted at the shoulders, hanging loosely to just below the knees. Long coat skirts divided into back and side vents to hip level. The coat closed down the front from neck to hem with a close row of buttons, but often left open to reveal the waistcoats. The necklines were usually without collars.

Large openings for pockets, horizontal or vertical, were low on the coat, and buttoned to prevent sagging. Sleeves followed doublet styles. Those short to the elbows had deep cuffs fastened to the sleeves by a button at the top.

By the late 1680s coats became closer fitting with a slight waisting. Sleeves became longer, almost to the wrists with turned-back cuffs. By the 1690s coats were better fitting at the waistline, the skirts flared, with pleats sewn in the side vents. They were seldom closed as the fashion was to reveal the waistcoat worn beneath.

Pockets were raised to just under the waistline. Shoulder knots, bunches of looped ribbons were worn on the right shoulder and were the forerunner of the later fashion for the profusion of ribbon bows and loops.

Waistcoats

Waistcoats became fashionable in the middle of the seventeenth century and were worn under doublets. After the late 1660s they followed the style and cut of the coats, but with closer fitting and longer sleeves. The cuffs were often turned over the coat cuff. As the back of the waistcoat was hidden beneath a coat, it was often made of a cheaper and inferior material. Such waistcoats were known as 'cheats'.

Outdoor wear

Jerkins, previously so popular, finally became unfashionable in the early 1630s. They were generally sleeveless, with the armholes covered with wings. Sham hanging sleeves were purely decorative.

Ruff made in flattened figure of eight set

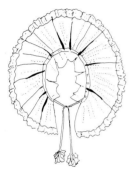

Lace edged falling band collar

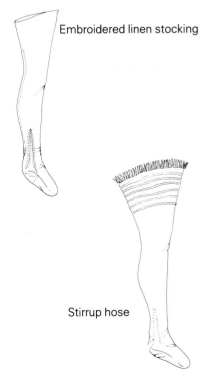

Falling band ruff, 1620-1640

Embroidered linen stocking

Stirrup hose

A military style *buff coat* or jacket was of leather. It was close fitting with a high waistline, the overlapping skirts reaching to just below the hips. It was sometimes slit to the waist at the sides and back. The collarless neckline was usually hidden by a large falling-band lace collar which matched the cuffs of the sleeves. These coats were generally only fastened at the waist, and were sleeveless. Sham hanging sleeves were sometimes attached, and beneath the welts were occasionally sewn sleeves of a soft contrasting material giving the impression of an under-doublet.

Until the early 1620s a loose thigh-length *mandilion* was still worn. A popular overcoat at the beginning of the century was a cassock, which was tent-like with a vent at the back. In the early part it reached the hips, gradually lengthening to thigh length. The loose sleeves had turned back cuffs. The fastening was with lace or buttons. Narrow standing collars were worn until the 1620s when collars disappeared, or became flat and turned down. A *gabardine* was another similar style, long and loose with wide sleeves. A *Brandenburg* – named after the Prussian city famous for its wool – was also a loose fitting winter coat, generally trimmed with cord and fastened with frogging.

Until the late 1660s cloaks in all styles were fashionable, the *manteau à la rietre* surviving until the late 1670s. These were then replaced by overcoats.

Neckwear and wristwear

Large *ruffs* became unfashionable by 1620, smaller and falling ruffs still being worn in the 1640s. *Falling ruffs* were formed by several layers being sewn to a neckband and fastened with bandstrings. *Falling bands* were worn throughout the period but entirely replaced ruffs in the 1640s to 1670s. They were separate collars, made of linen or cotton, usually lace edged, gradually increasing in size and falling to the shoulders. From the 1660s neckcloths were beginning to be worn. These remained popular to the middle of the nineteenth century and were later known as *cravats*.

Wrists had matching ruffs made in a similar way to the falling bands. Shirt sleeve cuffs were adorned with frills throughout the period.

Legwear

The various styles of trunk hose gradually evolved into breeches – hose gradually becoming synonymous with stockings.

Trunk hose with canions were popular until the early 1620s. They were in various styles as mentioned previously. Eyelet holes at the skirts of the doublets and similarly at the waist of the hose were joined together with ribbon ties, that could be hidden or decorative.

Cloak bag breeches, popular from the 1620s to 1630s were similar, being gathered at the waist, but not as full. They were highly decorated with points and embroidery.

Spanish hose or long-legged breeches reached from a high waistline to just below the knees. They were shaped to the body but were full in the seat. They could be closed with garters or bows just below the knees, and were allowed to overhang the stockings. At about hip level vertical slits or placket holes were the forerunner of modern pockets.

Rhinegrave or petticoat breeches with a short skirted doublet. The breeches are so wide that they give the appearance of divided skirts. They are profusely decorated with ribbon loops, c 1660

Open *breeches* were similar to the long-legged variety, but were wider, and the precedent to the extreme fashions of the petticoat breeches of the late 1670s. These were extremely wide, being attached in pleats to a waistband and falling below the knees. Due to their extreme fullness they could be mistaken for divided skirts, especially as a loose lining was allowed to hang below the breeches, giving the illusion of a petticoat. They were profusely decorated with ribbon loops. In the final decade of the century, plain closer fitting breeches were worn.

Although still tailored, the fashion for knitted stockings became general. Stockings were often lavishly embroidered, clocks designed to reach from ankle to calf. In order to make the legs more shapely, fashionable men often padded the calf to give a better line.

From about 1660, the Restoration, the words hose and stockings became interchangeable. Hose did not necessarily mean breeches. Hose were knitted in silk for the fashionable, wool or cotton for the middle classes and were of tailored material for everyday wear.

Garters were worn to keep stockings in place. They were of ribbon loops or bows just below the knees. Plain garters were strips of material fastened with buckles, over which the stockings could be rolled. Boothose, until the 1680s, were of a thicker material and worn as overstockings as protection for the thinner and more delicate stockings. They often had ornamental and decorative tops that could be turned over boot tops. Stirrup hose worn throughout the century were similar to boothose, mainly used for horse riding, but were without soles, having a strap beneath to hold them down. The tops could be attached to breeches.

Cannons were ornamental extensions to stockings, especially when worn with petticoat breeches. They were often turned over the garters, falling in flounces below the knees.

The loose coat is fastened from neck to hem and has low pockets. The turned back sleeve cuffs reveal the full shirt sleeves. A plain lawn falling band collar is worn over the coat neck, c 1670

Footwear

Until about 1630 the toes of shoes were fairly rounded, becoming more squared. Cork was used extensively to make the soles thicker as well as for wedge heels, until heels made of wood or leather became popular in the 1600s. At first they were low, but as they became higher they were more elegant. Most heels were curved and due to their incorrect positioning, angled the shoes. *Shoes* were mainly of leather or cordovan, a Spanish leather, giving shoemakers the name of cordwainers.

In the early part of the century shoes were usually open at the sides with the uppers forming tongues and the shoes secured with ankle straps tied with ribbon. Until about 1615 slashings were seen at the top to allow the stockings or linings to be seen.

Shoe roses made of ribbon loops, lace or leather were quite common, gradually becoming very elaborate, often encrusted with jewels. As *vamps* became higher and plainer, slashings disappeared and tabs became high to accommodate the large rosettes. Shoe buckles also became fashionable, made of metal and jewelled. During the Puritan period (1649-1660) shoes were plainer and lower heeled with less decorative buckles with a leather strap threaded through.

With the return of Charles II in 1660, shoe fastenings again became more delicate with curved Louis heels.

Petticoat breeches trimmed with ribbon loops. The short doublet has a falling band collar, *c* 1660

Doublet with puffed and paned sleeves ending in a small ruff. The neckline also has a falling ruff collar. The trunk hose and canions are worn with high soft leather boots, *c* 1625

Bucket boot with a stirrup guard and spurs

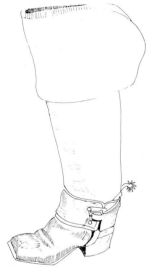

Postillion boot in stiff black leather with square toes. The heels are made of several layers of leather, the top of the boots turned back. Spurs were worn for riding and walking, c 1660

Puritan style felt hat with a wide brim. The narrow hatband has a buckle in front. A falling band is worn around the neck, c 1640

Pumps, shoes with soles that were thin and soft uppers, were worn for dancing, but also by footmen as part of their uniform. Boots, first worn mainly for riding, gradually became popular, and were made of softer leather. They were close fitting and fastened at the sides with lacing. They were often thigh length and fastened to the breeches by points. The tops were often folded over and the deep turned-down cuffs were extremely ornate, even to the point of having lace edging to match that on the clothes. Occasionally they would conceal perfumed sachets.

Bucket boots, popular from mid-century were more funnel shaped and shorter; the tops that folded down were known as bucket tops. These were usually of a firm leather and lined with material in beige or white. They were stiffened, although allowed to form folds around the ankles.

Postillion boots were generally of a thick black leather with spurs attached by leather links to a decorated boot guard. Spurs were worn by the fashionable men for walking as well as riding from about 1610 to 1660. Small shoes or slippers were sometimes worn inside boots to protect the feet from the thick leather of the boot. Mules or *pantoffles* were worn indoors and in fine weather only as they were made mainly of delicate materials. Metal edged pattens were still worn. *Gamashes* or leggings worn on horseback or by pedestrians as a protection against dirt were of material and fastened over the legs by buttoning. *Spatterdashes*, from the 1670s, were worn like garters to make shoes look like boots. Where they met the shoes large spur leathers were worn, thus covering the join, giving the appearance of boots.

Headwear

The *copotain* with its high conical crown and turned up brim continued to be worn in the first part of the century. From the 1640s to 1670 another similar style, the sugarloaf hat with a cone shaped and usually flat crown was worn, the brim often decorated with feathers. From the late 1600s low crowned, wide-brimmed boater shaped hats, also adorned with feather decoration, became popular. Another similar type was the Monmouth cock, worn at an angle. After about 1675 feather adornments were replaced by braid edging around the brim. In the last decade the tricorne became fashionable. This was a hat with the brim cocked in three equal proportions, forming a triangle with one point to the front and decorated with ostrich feather tips, the brim being edged with braid.

Caps ceased to be popular towards the middle of the century, usually only being worn by the older men or shop keepers.

Nightcaps were often made of brocade or fine materials, and were deep crowned made in four pieces forming a dome shape with turned up brim. They were worn indoors especially to cover a shaven head when the wig was removed.

Hairstyles

By 1620 the relatively short hairstyle was becoming longer. It was generally parted at the back with ringlets down to the shoulders. By the 1630s fringes brushed to one side also became fashionable. As hair grew in length beards and moustaches became less popular. The Puritans were clean shaven with short hair, the Extremists even cropping their hair very

Monmouth cap, round crowned and brimless, worn until the mid seventeenth cnetury

Shoulder length hair and a vandyke beard and moustache in the style of Charles I, c 1680

Wig with a centre parting, c 1661

Elaborate wig falling in curls over the shoulders and a neckcloth made of layers of lace, c 1680

close to the head, hence they were known as Roundheads. The Royalists, on the other hand, wore extremely long curly hair, the ringlets falling shoulder length were sometimes tied with ribbons and bows. Beards and moustaches were still seen in the first half of the century. Moustaches were waxed to curl up; beards were usually short and curly. They could also be pointed in the Vandyke style which became unfashionable after the fall of Charles I (1649). After the Restoration face patches again became popular, especially amongst the fops. These were first worn by men in the early part of the seventeenth century. Charles II (1660-1685) introduced a thin hairline style of moustache. Beards went out of fashion when periwigs became the mode. Wigs began to gain in popularity in Charles II reign. They were mainly made of goats and horse hair as well as real hair. The early wigs had the hair sewn on a close-fitting silk cap, but when wig-making became more important, strands of hair were individually threaded and knotted on to a canvas base. As wigs were heavy and uncomfortable hair was generally cut very short or shaven off entirely.

At first wigs were with centre partings and hair hanging down in curls either side. By the 1670s they became more elaborate and very cumbersome.

Large formal wigs with curls were called *periwigs*, and there were such names as full-bottomed wigs which were massive, with a centre parting and curls that framed the face, and hanging to the shoulders. From about 1675 the campaign wig was worn. This was bushy and shorter than the full-bottomed wig, with a queue or short tail tied at the back. This style was popular amongst the military who wore them with their breastplates from about 1680. They were issued with one pound of flour per week with which to powder them. The officers were issued with two pounds as their wigs were more elaborate.

Wigs became so cumbersome that many tied the hair back at the nape of the neck. By the 1690s these wigs had become so large that they were divided into three, the sides hanging over the shoulders and the other at the back. It was also fashionable to have the wig waist length and the left side could be longer than the right.

From the late seventeenth century powdered and scented wigs became the mode, worn by men and boys of all ages. A small linen cap to absorb the perspiration was usually worn between the head and the wig.

Periwigs became so popular by the end of the seventeenth century it was dangerous for children to go out unaccompanied, as it was common for them to be enticed in order to cut their long hair for the use of manufacturing these wigs. Wig-snatching also became a common form of theft. Earth clay was the best hair powder, but so expensive that most men were content to use ordinary flour perfumed and sometimes coloured blue. *Exquisites*, especially, preferred the blue colouring.

Gauntlet glove with embroidery around the thumb and edging ending with a fringe

Accessories

Gauntlet *gloves* were fashionable from 1595 until about the 1630s. The gauntlet part was generally made of six to eight pieces with either scalloped or fringing at the edge. Mittens with a compartment for finger and thumb usually had gauntlets. Plain gloves in soft leather had small turned-down cuffs revealing the coloured lining. Perfumed gloves were still fashionable. Fine lace-edged *handkerchiefs* were carried, some with buttons or tassels on the corners for decoration. These were fashionable until the 1670s.

Muffs made of satin or silk and later of fur, were first quite small, until the 1630s when they became large and were hung from a ribbon around the neck, or attached to a waistbelt or coat button.

Snuff boxes became very popular in silver or porcelain, the designs on these often being repeated on shoe decoration. Perfume, make-up and face patches were all employed by fashionable men.

Earrings, either worn on both or just one ear, became fashionable until about 1660. Rings, chains with pendants and lockets were also worn. Beard boxes were worn at night to preserve the shape of the beards.

Sleeveless leather vest with a double row of buttons to the waist and flapped pockets, *c* 1680

The leather buff coat fastened from the collarless neckline to the waist. The elbow length sleeves allow a softer leather sleeve to emerge to the wrists. From the waist down, the back and sides are slit, *c* 1635

Eighteenth century

The more efficient methods of production which resulted from a standardisation in the clothing trade had a marked effect on men's fashions in the eighteenth century. Before the French Revolution of 1789 costume styles were established by the aristocratic French. Men's dress remained fairly constant, the main changes being in the cut. Plainer materials were being used for everyday wear whilst the more elaborate brocades and silks were for dress or court wear.

Double-breasted coats were worn mainly by the lower class or for riding. Suits basically consisted of a frock or coat, waistcoat and breeches.

Collarless calf length coat buttoning from collar to hem, worn over a single-breasted waistcoat and cravat. The hat is a tricorne, *c* 1740

Coats

In the early part of the eighteenth century coats varied in length. They were close fitting and waisted with the skirts fully flared and three vents, one either side and one at the back at hip level. Until around 1720 the side vents had five to six pleats which were then reduced to three or four. Occasionally buttons were sewn inside the pleats, just leaving enough gap for a sword to be worn. The pleats were also stiffened with buckram to give a better flare. The back vent was unpleated until about 1730 when an inverted pleat became popular. Hip buttons of the same material as the coat itself were used as decoration at the top of the side vents where the pleats were stitched. Until about 1765 the coats were without collars, but from that date standing collars were seen. The collar could encircle the neck or have a small step under the chin.

Originally, the front of the coats hung straight with a slight overlap when closed. From the 1730s the fronts curved back slightly, so that the side seams, previously cut straight, also curved back thereby bringing the hip buttons closer together at the back. Coats were buttoned from neck to hem until the fronts were curved from which time they were only closed to just beneath waist level. By the 1760s flared skirts had disappeared and by the 1790s the coat tails ended at the knees and were square cut.

Back view of coat with full stiffened side pleats. The round closed cuffs curve round the elbows, *c* 1755

Buttonholes, made long, were sewn together leaving an opening just large enough for a button to pass through. Sham buttonholes were sometimes seen on the opposite side, with the buttons.

From mid century buttons were mainly fastened at the waist only thus revealing the frilled shirt in front. Sham buttonholes became very popular as decoration, and if the coats were heavily embroidered and ornate, hooks and eyes were used as fastening giving an edge to edge closure.

The frock coat is without collar and lapels and embroidered down the edges as is the pocket flap. The waistcoat base is squared. The breeches fastened just below the knee with a buckle over the stockings, and the shoe buckles are similar in style, c 1775

The plain frock has a turned down collar and the front of the waistcoat cut back at the front, c 1786

Until about 1710 horizontal pockets with oblong flaps that had rounded edges were fashionable. Vertical pockets were also seen. The flaps on pockets became narrower and were decorated with buttons. Many pockets were sham, but from the 1780s these became fewer and the pockets placed just below waist level and welts around the openings. Until the 1750s there were no inside pockets. The slit pockets were placed vertically just in front of the side vents and were often without flaps, especially when worn by men who carried the tools of their trade inside the pockets.

From then on coats had vertical pockets and sleeves without cuffs, known as slit sleeves. These were close fitting to the wrists, with a vertical slit on the outside seam; they could be buttoned, but were more often left open to reveal the shirt sleeves. The sleeves could be turned back to resemble a small cuff. Open cuffs, also known as open sleeves, became very deep by the 1730s. The cuff wings curved to the elbow at the back and were attached to the sleeves with decorative buttons. As the bottonholes could be false the cuff was sewn to the sleeve. In the 1740s cuffs became lower, and by mid century were no longer in fashion. Round closed cuffs became more popular and were curved around the elbows. They became quite deep and were known as boot cuffs or boot sleeves. In the 1790s sham cuffs were seen. These were simply a row of stitching. The close-fitting sleeves were generally puckered at the shoulders from about 1790.

Frock coats

Before 1730 a frock was a loose coat with a flat turned-down collar. The working class wore frocks mainly to protect their clothes from dirt, whilst the wealthier wore them for riding. Frocks were made similar to coats, but more amply. The neckline and sleeves varied. The flat collar known as a cape could be lined in a contrasting colour and the sleeves had wide, deep, closed cuffs at the wrists until about 1750 when shorter sleeves without cuffs became popular. Buttons, usually of metal, fastened down the front.

From the 1750s frock coats with turned down collars were worn for sports and every day dress, but after about 1770 they were seen on all occasions, including court wear. They were known as *frock coats* and cut in elegant styles and were worn instead of coats. They were generally plain, trimmed with braid or frogging, and were shorter than coats. When worn on sporting occasions the skirts were turned back. At Court frock coats were more elaborately embroidered.

In the 1760s the collars varied from flat and rolled styles, becoming quite narrow in the 1770s, with short squared flaps either side. By the 1780s it was fashionable to have the back high and a turnover coming to a slight point in the front. From about 1785 stand-fall type collars became usual wear. Buttons fastened the frocks to just below waist level. The skirts curved towards the back which became narrower and by the 1790s these had become mere coat tails.

Until 1780 frock coats were mainly single-breasted and without lapels. After that date when the coats were double-breasted, lapels became more common. They were usually small with a button between them and the collar. In the 1790s lapels became wider and more rounded, and after 1796

Collarless waistcoat, *c* 1720

Sleeveless and collarless waistcoat, *c* 1748

Double-breasted waistcoat with a low standing collar and lapel, *c* 1780

the gap between lapel and collar was so large that the front buttoning was further apart. Buttons were usually of gold or silver, but after the 1770s when buttons became larger, steel or mother-of-pearl was used. Enamelled buttons were also popular.

Pockets had plain flaps, and after the 1780s buttons and sham buttonholes were no longer seen. Pockets inside linings became popular in the late 1770s, and were sometimes seen without outside pockets.

The round cuffed sleeves of the 1750s became more close fitting and it was common to have a row of three buttons on the upper edge. Most popular from about 1780 were short vertical slits at the wrists with a vertical flap that could be left partially open.

Waistcoats

Waistcoats, similar in cut to coats, were close fitting to the waist with the skirts stiffened with buckram and the vents unpleated. The skirts reached to above the knees and were always shorter than those of the coat.

For sportswear waistcoats were very short with hardly any skirts. After 1740 the back was made shorter than the front. The skirts sloped out from the top of the side vents making the base wide. The back vent could be open to almost shoulder height and laced or taped to fit the owner.

The parts of the waistcoat that were not visible beneath a coat – usually the back and the sleeves to elbow level were often made of a cheaper material. When intended to be worn without a coat they were of the same material as the rest.

In the early part of the eighteenth century waistcoats were without collars, and like coats curved away in the front to reveal the breeches.

Fastening was with buttons which matched those of the coat, but were smaller. They were seldom closed below the waistline. Heavily embroidered waistcoats were fastened edge to edge with hooks and eyes.

From the 1730s double-breasted waistcoats were the style. Lapels, when present, were formed by the edges of the waistcoat being turned back. Pockets, smaller than those on a coat, were usually horizontal with flaps. Until 1760 waistcoats had close fitting cuff sleeves that extended below those of the coat. They were slit at the wrists, and although with buttons and buttonholes, these were usually left undone. By the 1760s the waistcoats were generally sleeveless, but for a brief time, in the 1790s, sleeves were again worn. These were gathered at the shoulder seam.

In the 1760s the front skirts became shorter and were cut back and by the 1780s side vents went out of fashion, leaving the front skirts just as flaps. In the 1790s square waistcoats became fashionable.

Single-breasted waistcoats were usually only fastened at the waist, although buttons were present from the neck to the curved-away part below the waistline. This curve increased from the 1760s and from about 1770 small lapels were added to the V shaped collarless waistcoat.

The double-breasted waistcoats were often buttoned with one to four buttons and in the 1760s the wide overlap on the right was buttoned to a large lapel whilst the other side was hidden. Double-breasted waistcoats were seen less in the 1770s but by the 1780s they were again common with low standing collars and lapels. They had two rows of closely placed buttons spreading out towards the shoulders. The base of the waistcoat

High wig worn by the Macaronis with the queue turned up on itself, *c* 1774

Natural hair brushed back, late eighteenth century

Hedgehog or herrison hairstyle, the top and sides brushed out in spikes, *c* 1785

could be cut either square or with a wide cut-away. Very popular in this period was material with either vertical or horizontal stripes and sometimes a silk fringe edging to the lapels and front edges.

In the 1790s under-waistcoats came into vogue. They were invariably shorter than the over-waistcoats and had square cut bases. The collars were mainly of the shawl variety. They were closed with just two or three buttons and the material visible was of a brighter and better quality than the remainder. They were designed mainly for warmth, made of flannel or other warm materials sometimes with sleeves. These were known as camisoles.

Indoor wear
From the early part of the eighteenth century informal indoor garments became popular.

A negligée known as *banjan* was a loose knee-length type of dressing gown. The back had a short vent and the front was wrapped over and fastened with either hooks and eyes or buttons. The close-fitting sleeves were generally slit at the wrists. During the 1780s the banjan could also be worn out-doors. Another type of morning gown was long and loose, of the wrap-over style, and tied with a sash at the waist. The sleeves, also long and loose, could be rolled back at the wrists. These gowns were never worn as night attire, but merely for comfort instead of a frock or coat.

Outdoor wear
Greatcoats and surtouts were worn outdoors. They reached usually below knee level and were loose fitting. They were made in four parts, seamed beneath the arms and down the centre back. The flared skirts were cut in one with the top, there being no waist seam. Sometimes there was only one side vent, on the right, this being essential for the sword to protrude. A vent at the back was usual as the surtout was often worn when horse riding.

They usually had two collars, a large flat one, like a cape, beneath a smaller one that could be pulled up and buttoned close to the neck in inclement weather. Sometimes instead of the smaller collar there was a narrow upright band. Belts or half belts from the side seams were of the same material as the coats. The wide sleeves ending in round cuffs were decorated with buttons and buttonholes.

By mid century the cape-like collars sometimes consisted of two to three capes of varying lengths, the short top one often faced with velvet. Greatcoats that were double-breasted had lapels. These coats closed with large metal buttons to just below the waistline. The long full sleeves had round cuffs with buttons decorating the top border. The horizontal flapped pockets were set far back; vertical pockets were less common.

The *redingote* was also popular. This was a calf-length close-fitting gown fastened down the front and could be worn as a light overcoat.

A *spencer* without tails was a short coat like a jacket ending at the waist. It had buttons down the front and a stand-fall collar. The long sleeves ended in cuffs. This short coat or jacket worn from the 1790s, was worn outdoors over a frock or coat.

Cloaks remained popular, full and long, until the 1750s, after which date they were worn mainly by professional men and the military or for funerals.

The open coat is worn without a waistcoat and at the neck a loosely tied Steinkirk cravat. The stockings worn over the knees are held up with ribbon garters. The hat is decorated with ostrich feather tips. The gauntlet gloves seen on his left hand have a frilled edge, *c* 1693

The coat has large cuffs decorated with buttonholes and buttons. The hair is in a bag-wig style. The gartered stockings are rolled up above the knees over the breeches and the shoes have large oblong buckles, *c* 1757

They were gathered at the neck and fastened with a clasp. A back vent was necessary when they were worn for riding.

A short cloak, usually knee length, known as a *roquelaure*, with a single or double cape collar was cut in four to flare out. It was buttoned down the front and had a back vent when worn for riding.

Neckwear

Until the 1740s cravats were still popular. They were generally made of a band of linen or lawn and tied loosely around the neck with the ends under the chin, lace-edged or decorated with tasselled beads.

The *Steinkirk cravat*, so named after the Battle of Steinkirk in 1692, was originally a military fashion and worn with the front ends twisted and passed through a buttonhole or attached to the side of the coat with a brooch. This style remained popular until the 1730s, although it was still worn by the older generation until the 1770s.

A high stiffened neckband known as a *stock*, made of lawn or cambric, was popular from about 1735. This allowed the ruffled shirt to be displayed. This *stock* gradually increased in height so much that it had to be stiffened with pasteboard. The buckles were often of precious metals studded with diamonds. If worn at the back they were often hidden by the fashionable wigs. The Macaronis wore neckties that were strips of material with lace or tasslled ends and with an ornamental buckle closure front or back.

The *solitaire* worn from the 1730s to the 1770s was a black tie worn over a stock. It was mainly worn with a bag-wig. The broad black ribbon allowed the ends to be either tied or left to dangle in the front.

The working class often only wore a folded *neckerchief* around the neck. For recreation or informal occasions neckwear was not always worn, and the shirt was often left open at the neck.

Leg wear

Knee breeches were worn throughout the century. They were full with the top gathered on to a waistband. The wide legs narrowed towards the knees ending with a kneeband. The lower part of the outer seam was closed with three or four buttons.

Until about midcentury gartered stockings known as *roll-ups* were worn over the breeches to above the knees, and then rolled over garters fastened beneath the knees. These were popular until the 1750s. Garters were made of strips of woven silk, sometimes chequered or decorated with other designs. From about 1735 the kneeband below the knees was closed with a buckle fastening over the stockings. These buckles often matched those of the shoes and were at first quite small.

The back of the breeches had a small slit so that the fit could be adjusted with either lacing, or after about 1745, a strap and buckle. the waistband was deeper in the front. Closure was by buttoning down the front with buttons on the right and a strip of material with buttonholes sewn to the left side of the fly opening. Another method of closure was drop-down flap, known as a fall. This method was popular from about 1730. There were two types of fall closure – a small fall, a flap centre front fastened with buttons to the waistband, and a whole fall which was larger and was fastened to the side seams with another button at the centre top of the waistband.

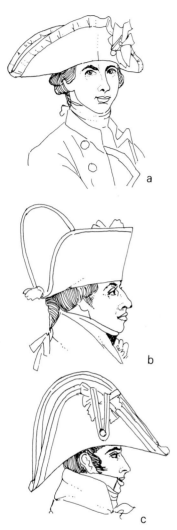

Pockets were generally at thigh level with flaps. These were horizontal and the flap was closed with a button to the waistband. Vertical pockets were placed in the side seams.

In the second part of the eighteenth century breeches were closer fitting and in the 1750s were shorter, exposing the knees. They again became longer in the 1760s, and were fastened beneath the knees with square buckles of all sizes. Towards 1778 the Macoronis popularised ribbon ties. these knee bands could be embroidered.

By the 1780s knee breeches became tight fitting and longer in the body and legs. Later brace buttons either side at the front and back were seen. *Braces*, known as *gallowses* were worn, as the breeches were no longer so tight-fitting at the waist and needed to be held up. At first braces consisted of a pair of leather straps passing over the shoulders and attached to the buttons on the breeches front and back.

Knee buckles were large and oval or oblong, but seldom round. They were worn vertically, and kneebands had a slight dip to accommodate them. From the 1790s pantaloons, a type of close-fitting tights ending at the ankles were worn. They buttoned on the outside to the calf and were pulled tight with a running string around the ankles. The top was closed with a fall.

Long overknee stockings were usually knitted, either by hand or machine. Clock designs were often knitted in. Stockings were of cotton, wool or silk, and were in a variety of colours. In the 1780s vertical stripes were popular and by the 1790s zigzag patterns were also seen.

Thicker stockings were worn over thinner ones inside boots to protect the thinner ones from rubbing.

Footwear

Buckled shoes, similar to earlier styles but in more delicate designs, were worn. The tabs became higher and the heels more shaped. Red, still popular for heels, were mainly for Court or formal occasions. Most were made of cork or leather. Squared toes, with correspondingly squared high heels again became fashionable. The scalloped or square tongues were often lined in a contrasting colour, and, as shoes became rounder and more pointed again from the 1750s, the heels and tongues became low and smaller. The elegant square or oblong buckles, small at the start of the century, became larger after 1740. They were mainly of metal and could be decorated with jewels. *Pumps* were low heeled shoes with a thin supple sole fastened with a buckle over the tongue. They were mainly worn only by fashionable men.

For riding, half-boots or *jackboots* to just below the knees were worn. The heavy boots had square and blocked toes with matching square heels, but by the 1740s the squareness became less obvious. They had large bucket tops and broad spur leathers with star-shaped *rowels*. Lighter jackboots conformed better to leg shape, with a dip at the back of the knee to allow for easier movement.

Hussar boots, popular towards the end of the century were also called Hessian boots, originating from the German Principality of Hess. These were short riding boots to just below the knees, higher in the front with a tassel decoration. These were mainly black, with a coloured border on top.

The full wig had the front hair either side of the centre parting in peaks, *c* 1700

Full bottomed wig, one side falling over the chest, *c* 1715

Tie wig, *c* 1750

Other fashionable boots included top boots made of grained leather with the tops turned down. The turned-back cuffs were often of a white chamois leather. *Highlows*, calf-length boots laced in front, were mainly worn in the country and by the working class from about 1785

Spatterdashes were fastened on the outside with lacing or buttons and held on the feet with buckle strap under the instep. They could be worn in place of boots for riding, but were mainly a military fashion. Overshoes or clogs were made to match shoes. Wooden-soled *pattens* with metal rings were worn from the second half of the seventeenth century to the Victorian period, mainly by the poorer class.

Headwear

Due to the extensive wearing of wigs, hats were seen less frequently. However, there were various styles meant to be carried rather than worn, such as the *chapeau bras*, similar to a flattened tricorne. The *Kevenhuller* was a variation of this shape, the front peak being pinched in. The Macaronis often wore small versions of three cornered hats, trimmed with feathers. These were often perched on their high wigs. Flat-crowned hats with rigid brims were worn by professional men, whilst the soft brims were more popular amongst the younger men and the middle class. Beaver was a very popular material for hats.

For riding, *jockey* caps were popular. They were round and had flat peaks in front. The bicorne, worn from the 1780s, had the brim turned up front and back, completely hiding the crown. The brim was pressed in at the front to form a peak, and was decorated on the left with a cockade or rosette. A hatband with a buckle in the front was also seen sometimes. Bicornes could also be worn for riding.

Hairstyles

Wigs became so large in this century that they were removed when indoors, and nightcaps were worn instead, as it was essential to cover the head that was mainly shaven or the hair cut very close. Pure white powder for wigs was introduced about 1703, although earth clay, which was cheaper than flour, and a combination of plaster of paris and starch as also used.

Grey and white were the most popular colours, although Macaronis preferred blues, pink, brown, etc – all perfumed. To make the powder adhere to the hair, it was first greased and the powder applied without bellows. Specially heated clay pipes in various sizes were used to curl the hair on wigs. There was a great variety in wig styles. Until about 1730 the full-bottomed wig continued in fashion from the previous century. This had the front hair in peaks either side of a centre parting. The peaks became lower after about 1710, and the mass of curls framing the face and falling below the shoulders, also became shorter after 1720, with the locks mainly behind.

Pigtails or *queues* were fashionable from the beginning of the century, they were convenient as the mass of hair was more manageable tied back. They were also known as tie wigs.

The curls could be held back with a black ribbon bow at the nape, or the hair could be plaited, interlaced with a black ribbon. Another practical

Calf length redingote without a side seam and narrow neckband hidden by a large bow. Over the tight fitting knee breeches are worn high soft leather boots. The hat is beaver and the muff of fur, *c* 1789

Coat with the flared skirts cut in one without a waist seam. There are three caped collars and a large lapel. The hessian type boots with the turned back cuffs in a contrasting colour, *c* 1786

and fashionable method was the bagging which held the hair in a black bag tied with drawstrings at the nape, finished with a large bow.

The variety of wigs was endless. In the second part of the eighteenth century wigs with queues became smaller as curls were worn less. A toupée, fashionable in the 1750s and 1760s had the front hair brushed straight back with horizontal curls just above the ears. From the late 1760s the front hair could be raised on pads. The toupée, either egg shaped or fanned out on the top, came straight down without sloping to the back of the head. The Macaronis wore large versions of a catogan or club wig, popular from the 1760s. This had a broad flat queue turned up on itself and tied in the middle with a black ribbon.

Shortly before wigs went out of fashion the hedgehog or herrison cut enjoyed a brief period of popularity. This had the top and sides brushed out in spikes and was either worn as a wig or styled from the natural hair itself. From the 1790s the natural hair was cut short in a variety of styles, from short crops to chin or shoulder length hair.

The Brutus crop, one of many fashions, was a short frizzy windswept style.

Accessories

Until about 1730 longer *gloves* were worn; they were made similar to the short ones, but could be fringed. Mittens were also still popular. *Muffs* remained popular, made in a variety of materials such as feathers and furs, often ribbon trimmed. From about 1740 small wrist muffs were worn both for warmth and protection of the shirt wrist ruffles.

Snuff boxes remained in fashion and were carried in waistcoat pockets. The insides of the lids often mirrored, the outside having a painted miniature, or of precious metal, tortoiseshell, ivory, etc.

Canes came into fashion early in the century, either long or short. The ornate head often carved could be detachable and hold scent or other small items in the hollow. Sticks were also popular from the 1730s. Both these items could have a ring attachment and looped to a coat button or to a finger for carrying.

Fob pocket watches were carried in the waistband pocket of breeches. The watch case was often of tortoiseshell or precious metal and through the ring handle short ribbons could be attached to a key chain and the waistband. The Macaronis used a great deal of perfume and make-up – they even carried small combs for their eyebrows.

Face patches remained popular as a fashion accessory as well as covering up skin blemishes.

To enhance their legs, gentlemen resorted to pads and bandages to give the calves a better line.

Nineteenth century

Double-breasted coat with the front sloped to form two tails square ended. The deep lapels have an M notch. The sleeves are gathered and padded at the shoulders. The waistcoat has a high stiff collar, *c* 1807

The single-breasted overcoat with an M shaped notch between collar and lapel is worn over a frock coat and two waistcoats square cut in the front. The pantaloons are tucked into knee high buskin boots with a large turn-down in a different colour. The tall hat is of beaver, *c* 1803

Coats

Skirted coats were worn throughout the first half of the nineteenth century. The coat tails at the back were divided by a vent and had pleated tops ending with hip buttons. There were either pockets in the pleats or a flapped pocket each side of the skirt at waist level. The flaps were mainly rectangular, but were scalloped for Court wear. The front skirts ended at the waist and met the back tails horizontally – similar to present day dress coats. Another fashion had the fronts curving down from the last button to the back. This style resembled the contemporary morning coats.

The notch between the stiff stand-fall collars was V or M shaped. The M was popular until about 1855 for everyday wear and persisted into the 1870s for evening wear. Coat sleeves were either cuffed at the wrists or had side slits closed with two buttons.

There were several coat styles, single or double breasted. On single-breasted styles the fronts sloped away from the waist and the tails were rounded. The two or three buttons were mostly metal plated for day wear whilst for evenings they were flat gilt; the coats themselves were mainly dark blue. On double-breasted styles the fronts overlapped with a double row of buttons, one for fastening. The front skirts were either square or rounded and the tails at the back squared. The sleeves were plain and the collar was lapelled.

High stand-fall collars and sleeves gathered and padded at the shoulders was a *French* style named after Jean de Bry.

From about 1820 most double-breasted coats had a separate piece of material for the buttons and buttonholes known as a *button stand*. This took the strain from the bulk of the material when the coat was buttoned up.

The coat body had only three seams, one either side and one centre back, with the side seams set towards the back. As the coats were made to fit tightly for evening wear they were almost impossible to close, thus revealing the waistcoat, shirt and cravat. In order to give a better fit a dart or separate piece of material was inserted under the armholes to the waist giving the coat five seams and six pieces of material.

In the early part of the century the collar was large and stiff, lined with buckram. The front of the coats were often padded. The waist-high pockets could be concealed in pleats or be flapped.

The single-breasted cut-away square-ended frock coat had tails. The collar and lapels are separated by a notch, and the sleeves padded and gathered at the shoulders. The waistcoat has stiff standing lapels. The pantaloons have a small fall opening in the front. The top hat has a turned up brim, *c* 1803

Frock coats

Frock coats were first seen around 1816 and were single-breasted, buttoning from neck to waist. The collar was rolled or in a stand-fall style known as a *Prussian collar*. They were generally of military style. The fitted bodice was joined at the waist to straight full skirts with a vent at the back. The length of coat varied, but in the 1820s the waist was lengthened. Sleeves had a slit or were cuffed at the wrist and had a gathered kick-up at the shoulders. To keep the military image, frogging or braid was often used as decoration. By the 1830s frock coats were the most popular wear for informal occasions; they ended at about the thigh. High collars, wide lapels and front padding were popular. Hip pockets were hidden under flaps or between pleats, a breast pocket sometimes being seen.

There were several styles: the *petersham frock* coat was double breasted with a double row of four buttons and a broad velvet collar with lapels and cuffs to match. The *Taglioni frock* was single-breasted with a narrow collar and lapels. The skirts were fairly short and full. From the 1840s the Taglioni had side bodies and sometimes a Prussian collar of the stand-fall type. Like the coats the frock coats had side bodies inserted on each side under the arms to give better fit. Double-breasted styles also had button stands. By the 1850s the surtout became indistinguishable from the frock coat, being worn for formal and informal wear. After 1850 they were less waisted, allowing the skirts to hang straighter.

In the late 1850s short frocks with fairly small collars and lapels became fashionable. Double-breasted frocks had four pairs of buttons whilst the single breasted ones had only two. Braid edgings were popular.

From the early 1870s single-breasted frocks were more fashionable and buttoned high, concealing the waistcoat beneath.

Frock coats became less popular from the 1880s, being replaced by morning coats.

Tail coats

In the 1820s tail or morning coats were usually double breasted whereas for evening wear they were generally single breasted. The collar was high at the back and low in the front, and joined to the rolled lapel with a V or M notch. When the coats were double-breasted the lapels were large, but when single-breasted they were smaller. The coat body was square at the waist with short wide tails.

The pleats of the skirts were often decorated with buttons. From about 1824 sleeves were gathered and padded at the shoulders, known as leg-o'-mutton. By the late 1840s this fashion had become less popular.

From the mid 1800s single- or double-breasted tail coats were worn formally for day or evening wear as well as for riding. They were also known as *dress coats* or *swallow-tail coats*. The coat tails reached the knees and were slightly rounded. Collar and cuffs often velvet trimmed with slit or closed cuffs decorated with two buttons. Pockets were concealed in the pleats and closed with four buttons for day wear but were left open when worn for evening attire. The top of the left lapel often had an extra buttonhole to hold a flower.

When worn on dress occasions the sleeves and skirts were satin or silk lined. For day wear the dress coats were cut back just below waist level and the tails cut square, reaching to almost knee level.

By the end of the 1860s the coats were worn mainly just for livery or everyday wear. They were usually black.

In the early 1880s the dandies of the period popularised a new style of coat. It was tight-waisted and the low, rolled collar merged with the lapels which were faced with corded silk. The cuffs were stitched and ended with one button. However, by about 1893 the stepped roll collar was again seen and the shoulders became more square, with the coat skirts getting slightly longer, and cuffs without buttons. The skirts gradually became more spoon-shaped and tapered. The lapels came so low that only two buttons were necessary.

Morning coats

In the early nineteenth century morning and riding coats were tail coats with the front edges sloped instead of straight cut. They were mainly single-breasted with large collars and lapels. The coats could also be of the *Newmarket* style. They had pleated back vents with a hip button. Flapped pockets and outside breast pocket were also sometimes seen. For riding the favourite colour was dark green, whilst for hunting scarlet was worn.

The Newmarket, or riding coat, also known as a *cut-away*, by 1870 merged into a morning coat. The skirt had short rounded corners and the sleeves were cuffed. The hip pockets were often flapped.

Morning coats were similar in cut to the dress coat, even when fashions altered. These coats, either single or double breasted, were worn open or with just the top button fastened.

Turned-down collars sometimes were without lapels, rolled collars often had lapels.

Sleeves usually had slit cuffs.

Another style, the *Doncaster*, had fuller skirts and the coat generally was looser fitting.

In the 1850s morning coats still resembled frock boats, but the fronts sloped away to form broad tails, and the edges were usually bound. They were generally single-breasted with pockets in the pleats, or at the waistline in which case they were flapped. There could be a breast pocket on the left.

In the 1860s, the morning coat with the fronts less curved were often called shooting coats. Longer waists before the mid 1860s necessitated five buttons in the front, but when the waist became shorter only two or three buttons were required. With the shorter waistlines curves again became more prominent, the front reaching the knees and being rounded or square cut.

Sleeves were peg-topped becoming close fitting in the 1870s.

The pockets were hidden by flaps at the waist. The edge of the coat was bound or corded and the collars were velvet faced. Single-breasted morning coats had square skirts with three buttons in the front, only one being closed, and, as the waistline lowered, single-breasted styles

Single-breasted Taglioni frock with a narrow collar and lapels. The skirts are joined at the waist. The trousers are straight all the way down, *c* 1864

The tail coat has a low collar joined to the lapel with an M notch. the pantaloon trousers are wide ending above the ankles, *c* 1819

Full evening dress. The tail coat has a continuous roll collar and the waistcoat is low cut. The stiff shirt front could be a false front, known as a dicky, c 1894

Morning or dressing gown with a shawl collar faced in the same material as the sleeve cuffs. The cord around the waist is tasselled, c 1873

became the more popular, often being worn in place of frock coats. Double-breasted fancy waistcoats were generally worn with the coats. The plain unpadded sleeves ended in stitched-down cuffs with two buttons.

Lounge and informal jackets

From the late 1830s lounge jackets were worn informally, generally with matching waistcoats and trousers. The jackets were better fitting than those of the previous century as the side seams had a dart from under the arms, slightly forward towards the waist. The jackets were mainly single-breasted with the skirts just covering the seat. They seldom had back vents, but were seamed at the waist and had side pleats with hip buttons. The fronts were slightly curved. Collar and lapels were fairly small and the pockets either side were at waist level. On the left breast a handkerchief pocket was usual. Sleeves were generally straight, but became peg-topped around 1858.

At about this time the *Tweedside* lounge jacket originated from Scotland. This was single-breasted buttoning high to the neck with only the top three or four buttons closed. It was loose fitting without a seam down the centre back. The collar was small, and the lapels were short. Patch pockets were general. About 1861 the fit of the jacket was improved with the insertion of the side bodies.

About 1862 a double-breasted style of lounge jacket became known as *reefer* or pea jacket; this was short with a low collar and short lapels as well as side vents. The pockets were either flapped or of the patch variety, the edges bound or braided. Reefer jackets could also be worn in winter as overcoats. By about 1870 they became less popular although a single-breasted version did become fashionable around 1878 amongst the younger generation. They had a short roll collar and were buttoned high. The fronts were square cornered.

In the 1860s *The Prince of Wales* jacket, became popular. There was a looser version of a reefer with three rather than four pairs of buttons. The pockets were flapped over the opening or the opening could be braided. Also very fashionable in the same period was another style of jacket known as a *Norfolk* jacket. This was mainly worn in the country. It buttoned high to the neck, and had a box pleat centre back and two box pleats in the front. There were two flapped pockets either side, and the belt around the waist was of the same material as the jacket. These jackets were often worn with knickerbockers and deerstalker hats, although from the 1880s they were also worn with bowlers. From about 1894 Norfolk jackets tended to be yoked, with the box pleats emerging from the yoke.

In the 1880s single-breasted lounge jackets had rounded corners and reached the bottom of the trouser seat. The jackets were fastened with four or five buttons and had four outside pockets including a ticket pocket. The sleeves were just short enough to reveal the fashionable shirt cuffs and the sleeve cuffs were formed by a double row of stitching and had three buttons and buttonholes.

In the 1890s the jackets tended to be left open, and about 1895 only three buttons were considered fashionable. It was also not necessary to have a centre seam down the back. By about 1898 the *lounge jacket* was the most

PLATE 3   Left *The top hat, made of black silk, is worn over a short hairstyle. The morning coat has short revers and fastens with three buttons above the waist. The short collar is stiff and high, worn with a cravat. The pin-striped trousers flap over the shoes, c 1900.   Centre back The informal cut-away coat has M-shaped revers and square ended tails. The pantaloons are buttoned up at the sides and strapped beneath the shoes, c 1807.*

Centre *A coloured beaver top hat is worn over the curly hair with full side whiskers and beard. The single-breasted frock coat is thigh length with a flared skirt, c 1857.   Right Victorian dandy. The single-breasted jacket is short and loose with a rounded collar, worn over a waistcoat. The jacket is bound in braid, and the contrasting loose trousers are in a check material, c 1870*

PLATE 4   Left *Plus-four suit worn with a flat golf-style cap.*
The shirt has a soft collar and is worn with a tie. A knitted
cardigan replaced a waistcoat. The shoes are brogues and the
woollen knitted socks are held up with fringed garters,
c 1928.   Centre front *Single-breasted lounge suit consisting*
of matching jacket waistcoat and trousers with turn-ups. The
hat is a snap-brim trilby, c 1932.   Background *Single-*
breasted morning coat with narrow trousers with turn-ups. The
shirt has a butterfly collar, and a bow tie is worn. The hat is a
bowler, which replaces the popular silk top hats, c 1914.   Right
The Norfolk jacket is yoked and pleated with patch pockets
and knickerbockers. Leather gaiters are worn with the boots.
The matching cape is of a chesterfield pattern and reaches just
below the knees, held in position with straps, c 1906

Double-breasted waistcoat with braid edgings, 1850s

Waistcoat with pockets, 1870s

Waistcoat with top pocket, 1870s

Waistcoat with a rolled collar, 1870s

popular form and also became known as a *dinner jacket*. Dinner jackets were worn informally for dinners, parties and theatres. They had roll collars in one with the lapels ending at waist level, and were faced in silk. There were just one or two buttons and buttonholes.

Waistcoats

Waistcoats were one of the most fashionable and decorative items in a man's wardrobe and were often made of richly embroidered materials.

Single- or double-breasted waistcoats with or without collars and revers were usually waist length. Until about 1825 they were generaly square cut, thereafter being slightly pointed at the centre front. They were generally single-breasted and square cut, just being visible from beneath the coat in the early part of the century. Of the five or six buttons, the upper ones were often left open to reveal the frilled shirt front. The fronts were slightly padded and a dart under the lapel and armhole also helped created the fashionable fullness.

The rolled collar and lapel had no notch and ended at the second or third button. Both collar and lapel could be of a different colour. Low stand collars were also seen.

Waistcoats usually had two pockets low down and occasionablly a crescent shaped one higher up to hold a pocket watch. For day wear the single-breasted waistcoats had roll collars and lapels, large enough to fold over the coat. The eight buttons were generally covered in the same material as the waistcoat. Waistcoats were often corded at the edges and the fronts at the base could be leather lined.

After the 1850s waistcoat buttons ended slightly higher than previously, had six buttons, the lowest placed higher than previously. The pockets were generally welted and the watch was carried in its own pocket with the chain passing through a buttonhole. From about 1853 double-breasted styles became popular for morning wear and when worn with single-breasted frock coats lapels became wider and the points buttoned back. Fastening was with three or four pairs of buttons.

From the early 1850s waistcoats were made to match the trousers and a little later also the jackets. The back of the waistcoat was often of a lining material as it was not visible. Tapes or buckles and strap behind were employed to give the waistcoats a better fit.

White single-breasted waistcoats were always worn for evening wear in the early 1800s. By the 1840s they were generally double-breasted and made of materials such as velvet or satin with embroidered designs. Some had small stepped or roll collars that were notched, the buttons being of self material or of precious stones. White waistcoats with five buttons were worn with the dinner jacket that first came into vogue in the 1880s.

For funeral wear waistcoats were black.

Underwaistcoats

Underwaistcoats often made of quilted material worn with sleeves for extra warmth as an undergarment. Early in the 1800s ornamental under waistcoats consisted of just two pieces of material joined at the back of the neck. When it became a complete garment, stand collars were attached. Towards the end of the 1820s the visible parts became more ornate with

Double-breasted Ulster coat with attached cape and half belt at the back. Bowler hat with a curved brim. Spats are worn over the shoes, *c* 1876

Riding coat with the front slightly sloped. The sleeves are gathered at the shoulders. The high pantaloons are worn with riding boots, the tops turned over and with spurs, *c* 1828

the protruding lapels in contrasting colour, the overwaistcoats being left open to reveal these.

Formal wear

For court wear single-breasted dress coats with the front panels curving back were worn at the start of the nineteenth century. They were mainly of embroidered velvet, dark greens, browns or blue being the most popular colours. White satin waistcoats and velvet or silk breeches were worn. The stockings were of white silk and the black shoes buckled. Bag wigs were the most popular and *chapeau bras* were carried.

By the 1840s single-breasted tailcoats with stand-up collars were fashionable. The pocket flaps, collar and cuffs often decorated in gold, and gold coloured buttons were sewn on to the white collarless waistcoats. Shirts were lace frilled. The white breeches had matching gold embroidery and the shoes were gold-buckled.

For full evening dress dark coloured single- or double- breasted dress coats were worn. The buttons were of gilt or self material. Pockets were concealed in the pleats, flaps covering the sham ones. Waistcoats were of velvet or silk, stockings white and breeches white or a pale colour until pantaloons or trousers came into fashion. These could be of a darker colour or black. By the 1850s waistcoats were black or white with decorated edges.

In the 1860s tight black trousers were the mode often with a stripe down the outer seam. When the dress waistcoat became unfashionable about 1880 a red or black silk sash was worn around the waist. Plain bow ties were worn, black for evening wear, but white for balls.

Black buckled shoes and pumps were worn, or patent leather boots with suede tops were also seen from the 1880s. Opera hats were carried. Dress gloves were a popular accessory. From the 1840s blue was the fashionable colour for weddings. The dress coat with gilt buttons could have a velvet collar.

Two waistcoats were worn and the underwaistcoat in the early 1800s was quilted, but later was of plain satin with a roll collar. The overwaistcoat of white velvet was later of a heavily embroidered damask. Breeches or pantaloons were light in colour until the 1840s when black was more fashionable. By the 1870s dress frock coats or morning coats were equally popular although the morning coats with light coloured trousers became the mode.

For mourning all the attire had to be black including neckties, gloves, stockings and even handkerchiefs had black borders. Black hatbands were obligatory.

The correct attire for morning wear in the 1890s was a single-breasted lounge or morning coat, a bowler with lounge suit or a silk hat with morning coat being usual. Coloured shirts with white collars were worn. Collars were fairly high. Striped trousers were worn at receptions.

Informal and sportswear

Indoors silk or brocade dressing or morning gowns were worn instead of a coat. They often had shawl collars, were loose fitting, wrapping over the front and were tied around the waist with a tassel ended cord. Often a

Velvet smoking jacket with quilted cuffs and roll collar, mid nineteenth century

Yoked Norfolk jacket and knee length knickerbockers. The woollen stockings are ribbed, c 1897

taselled skullcap or round nightcap and slippers were worn. By the 1830s dressing gowns were often of a patterned material and brightly coloured. Another type of morning attire was a *banjan* which was slightly waisted with a vent or pleat at the back with hip buttons.

Smoking jackets, worn from the 1850s were fairly short, usually made of velvet or quilted material. They had roll collars and were edged with cord. Fastening was generally with buttons and loops.

For riding, frock coats, pantaloons or breeches and hessian boots were worn. Tall hard-topped hats were usual. From about 1838 a riding coat known as a *Newmarket* was worn with breeches or tight trousers. By the 1870s a single-breasted lounge jacket and checked waistcoat with a vent could be worn. From the 1880s riding breeches were close fitting from the knees and were fastened on the outside with buttons. The insides were often faced with leather. Hunting coats were like short frock coats with deep flapped pockets at the waist as well as two on the inside. Waistcoats were often embroidered with hunting motifs. Long or half boots were worn with strapped trousers. Top hats or jockey caps were popular.

Short frock coats were worn for shooting. They were generally of a waterproof material and had many pockets. The fairly tight trousers were buttoned at the base and often waterproof ones were worn on top. By the 1870s *knickerbockers* were popular and by the 1880s Norfolk jackets were also worn. For yachting and boating short pea jackets as well as reefers were worn. Loose trousers, and later knickerbockers, were fashionable. White peaked hats and white canvas shoes were usual. Cravats worn loosely around the neck were fashionable for sporting activities.

In the 1870s short jackets and white trousers were worn for cricket. From about 1887 blazers became the correct attire for both cricket and tennis.

Football outfits consisted of striped jerseys, knickerbockers and stockings, whilst for golf, morning coats or Norfolk jackets were worn with either knickerbockers or trousers. Until the turn of the century *golf caps* were also worn. These were also worn for cycling as gentlemen often cycled to the golf courses.

Outdoor wear

At the beginning of the nineteenth century *greatcoats* or overcoats were columinous and reached the knee or ankles. They were usually single-breasted and buttoned to just beneath the waistline, the buttons being leather or material covered, and sometimes made of mother-of-pearl. The collar was high at the back and low front joined the lapels with a V or M notch. The back had either a vent or a slight overlap or pleat. Pockets were flapped at the hips and it was also usual to have inside breast pockets.

In the first decade straps as well as buttons were used as fastening. Coats became calf length and the collar lapels and cuffs were often trimmed with fur. Another style, a loose box shape, could be belted or fitted with a strap at the back. Various shoulder capes distinguished these coats which were originally worn on the box of a coach or cab as a driving coat.

A fitted coat, similar to a frock and worn from about 1818, was known as a *surtout*. There were various versions of greatcoats, some of which fastened with loops or frogs or Brandenburgs.

When Charles Mackintosh patented a waterproof fabric, outer garments

Yoked Raglan coat, *c* 1897

Inverness coat with the cape sewn into the seams. The hat is a deerstalker style, *c* 1880

made of this material grew in popularity. Amongst the many styles there were pilot coats, *Taglioni greatcoats* and *Petershams* with shoulder cape and spreading collar. In the 1840s the *Chesterfield* became one of the most fashionable of coats. It was closed with between four and five buttons hidden by a fly front. The turned over collar was in velvet with silk facings and narrow notched lapels. The pocket edges were braided and were just below the waistline. About 1885 coats could have detachable shoulder capes buttoned to the collar. The *paletot* or pilot coat was short waisted, resembling a frock coat. There were several variations; one, single breasted, had a hood instead of a collar, and double-breasted, loose-fitting version was similar to a Chesterfield.

From about 1859, the *Ulster*, an ankle-length overcoat had a detachable hood and was belted. More often it was double breasted. Sometimes the belt was just at the back and attached in the side seams.

An Albert overcoat reaching the calves, had a fly front opening with a semi-circular cape, and deep vent at the back.

A short double-breasted overcoat named after the Prime Minister Gladstone had a shoulder cape and was trimmed with astrakhan. Another style of short coat was a *covert* worn in the 1880s. This was like a short fly-fronted Chesterfield. By about 1897 the sleeves were of the Raglan style, named after Lord Raglan of Crimean War fame.

A raglan overcoat, popular at the end of the nineteenth century was cut on the cross. The side seams had a vent with the two holes so placed that it was possible to put the hands through and into the trouser pockets. The coat was closed with a fly front and was often of a waterproof material, gradually replacing the mackintosh of the 1820s. Cloaks were long and voluminous with slits sometimes covered with flaps for the arms to protrude. By the 1840s they were usually knee length and had small turned-down collars. Some had capes attached, and even sleeves. For evening wear capes often had large fur collars. Cloaks with wide sleeves became popular in the 1850s.

By the 1830s shoulder capes for travelling were shaped to fit the shoulders and neckline with a large turned-down collar.

In the 1860s an *Inverness cape*, was like a loose knee-length overcoat hanging from a fitted collar, sometimes with large pockets. Ten years later the Inverness cape was caught into the side seams of a coat by the sleeves; this was known as a dolman-sleeved style. By the 1890s the cape was close fitting. A raglan cape with sleeves of that name was like a loose overcoat. The sleeves came to a point at the top of the neck where they were joined to the front and back of the garment at the collar seam.

Neckwear

In the first half of the century especially, neckwear made an important contribution to fashion.

Shirt collars were high with the points extending to the cheeks so that neckcloths became wider and were starched. In the 1820s some shirt collars were separate and kept on with ribbon ties fastened at the back. The collars were deep enough to be turned over a cravat or tie. Different styles had names such as the *Piccadilly*, a stand-up variety, the *Dux*, similar but with the points in the front turned down. The *Shakespeare* was a standfall style with large points.

A la Byron neckwear

Double-breasted riding coat also worn formally with a silk top hat, c 1850

Long waisted overcoat and sleeves full at the shoulders, c 1829

Cravats were squares or triangles in a fine material and starched. The ends were tied in a bow or knot in front. For informal wear they were coloured or patterned but when worn formally, they were always plain white. They had a variety of names, such as the Ballroom, Hunting, Mailcoach and Napoleon. In the 1830s very large cravats or scarves spread over the shirt front and were fastened with an ornamental tie pin. Very small cravats became extremely fashionable in the 1840s, the ends fringed or lace edged. The *Byron*, named after the poet, was very narrow like a shoestring, and was usually worn with a turned-down collar.

Stocks became fashionable about 1822. They were shaped and stiffened neckbands fastening at the back with ties, buckles or hooks and eyes. They were generally black and in various styles, being worn formally as well as for sports.

In the 1890s neckties became very popular. There was great variety – from bow ties, to narrow lengths of material like a shoelace (known as string ties) and ties with knots at the neck and the ends hanging down one over the other. They were made in all kinds of materials and patterns. They could be bought ready made up, tied in the correct manner and fastened behind.

For evening attire butterfly bows in white piqué were usual.

Legwear

Until about 1810 *breeches* were worn for evening wear, although they were still worn by day until about 1830. They were usually of a lighter colour than the remainder of the suit. For sports, such as riding and hunting, breeches were worn throughout the century, made of soft leather. The front of the breeches still had fall closures, the front fly opening only being used from the 1840s, mainly for evening wear. In the first decade breeches were high-waisted and fairly full at the hips. They fastened at the knees or just below with either buttons or a buckle. After about 1824 the back of the breeches were tightened at the waist with a strap and buckle. Until the 1820s there was only one brace button each side of the front, but by the 1830s two buttons became commonplace.

Pantaloons were generally of a stretch material, sewn to a waistband with a vent at the back for a better fit, and a small fall or fly opening in front. They also had brace buttons at the waist. Pantaloons were made with just one outside seam until about 1810 after which date they were also seamed on the inside. After about 1817 the tight-fitting pantaloons ended at the ankles and were strapped under the foot to keep them taut. The slits at the ankles were closed with buttons or ribbon ties.

Pantaloons were worn mainly with hessian or half boots as well as Hussar buskins that reached the calves. Pantaloons were at first mainly worn for walking-out, but by the 1850s were worn more for riding and hunting.

Pantaloon trousers were not as tight-fitting, so did not need a slit at the sides, but they were still strapped beneath the foot to hold them down. Beau Brummel began a fashion for wearing black pantaloons for evening wear.

From about 1807 trousers were only worn for informal wear, and for evening wear from around 1817. They were almost straight all the way down the leg and ended just above the ankles. They were often of a striped material and were worn mainly with shoes, and sometimes gaiters. About 1817 trousers became longer, reaching the shoes, and until mid century had straps under the instep. The tops were gathered to a waistband and there were side pockets in the seam. They were tightened from the back with strap and buckle. Until about 1823 a fall opening was always used but by the 1870s all trousers had fly fronts.

About 1857 peg-topped styles came into fashion. The legs were wide around the hips tightening towards the ankles, matching the type of sleeves popular in this period. From about 1876 trouser legs were tight to the knees and then flared out. These were often worn with reefer jackets and were fashionable with the dandies of that time. Pockets placed horizontally became more popular than the side ones. A hip pocket was also introduced. Throughout the years trousers varied slightly in width.

By the 1890s trouser bottoms could be turned up and a trouser press was used to give a firm crease down the front. A new form of loose breeches known as *knickerbockers* was worn from the 1860s. They originated from the uniform of the Rifle Volunteers and were mainly for walking and sports generally. As they were baggy, a wide knee-band fastened with buckle and strap or buttons was often hidden beneath the voluminous material. Tweed was a popular material. Knickerbockers matched the Norfolk jackets with which they were often worn. As the century progressed knickerbockers gained in popularity.

Braces were attached by buttons one on each side of the front and at the back, each side of the vent, until about 1825. By about 1850 when the back vent was not so much in use, the buttons were sewn on two slightly raised points either side of the back seam. There were now generally two buttons on each side, front and back, so that braces had two bands which joined to form two V shapes. Brace buttons were usually of metal or bone. Braces were often embroidered and by the 1860s the fronts had double sliding ends, making them adjustable.

Underwear
Throughout the nineteenth century and into the twentieth century fashionable men wore corsets. They were similar to a lady's, made of whalebone. They were worn to accentuate the waist and puff out the chest.

Court dress coat sloping back. It is profusely decorated and has a stand collar. The shirt is frilled with lace. The breeches are buttoned and buckled at the knees and the low pumps are buckled, *c* 1803

Peg-topped trousers fastened with a fly front, mid nineteenth century

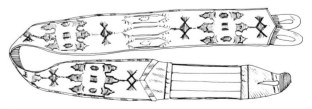

Embroidered braces, *c* 1850

Wellington breeches worn over boots, *c* 1820

Shoe with a spat buttoning up the side

Leather boots with buckles and strapped fastenings up the sides, *c* 1815

Footwear

In the first part of the century boots were very fashionable and were named after eminent people such as Wellington, Napoleon, Blucher. They were mainly military styles made of black calf, to the knees, but slightly lower at the back for easier movement. Spurs were worn on all occasions by the fashionable. Loops at the top on either side facilitated pulling on the boots which were also held up with boot garters attached at the back of the boots, and fastened above the knees. These styles with low square heels and rounded toes were generally worn with breeches. *Wellington boots* became fashionable about 1819 and *Bluchers*, a type of half boot, were popular just a little later. They were open in the front and fastened over a tongue.

By the later 1870s Wellington boots lost their popularity and were replaced by buttoned boots. By the 1880s patent and suede boots were worn for the daytime.

Hessian boots still remained popular from the previous century and were worn with pantaloons, Buskins were very similar, except they were slightly shorter and did not have the tassel decoration in the front. Highlows were another style still popular, especialy amongst the working class and for country wear.

By the 1830s heels became higher and toes were more pointed. In 1839 when vulcanized rubber was patented this was used extensively for the heels and soles of boots, shoes and even sports shoes with canvas uppers.

Elastic-sided boots with an insertion of elastic either side were popular from the 1840s until the end of the century. After the French Revolution in 1789 the popularity of buckles gradually declined. They were slowly replaced by laces. Pumps or dress shoes were worn at Court or on formal occasions. They were made of a specially treated leather that was varnished and lacquered until it shone – patent leather. *Spatterdashes* made of cloth and worn mainly with breeches reached just below the knees and were fastened on the outside with a row of buttons. Half gaiters or spats were shorter to just above the ankles and worn with pantaloons or trousers. They also buttoned on the outside edge, and had a strap passing under the shoe to hold them down. They were often of a canvas in either grey or fawn.

Overshoes such as galoshes or clogs were worn for inclement weather. About 1844 rubber galoshes were made to fit over the shoes.

For Court wear *stockings* were usually white with clocks, whilst for formal evenings they were flesh coloured in open work with embroidery.

By about 1820 ribbed stockings were popular, especially worn with knickerbockers and leggings. Coloured and striped stockings were also seen later in the century. *Half stockings*, another name for socks, were worn mainly on informal occasions.

Top hat with a small turned up brim, *c* 1819

Low-crowned wide-awake style hat with a wide turned up brim, *c* 1819

Wide-awake hat. The curly hair and side whiskers met

Tall crowned top hat with the brim turned up at the sides, *c* 1840

Headwear

There was a great variety of headwear, in the early part of the nineteenth century. Low flat crowns with curved brims were mainly for country wear whilst bowl shaped crowns with narrower curved brims were worn in town and were the forerunner of the present-day bowler hat. By the 1880s felt bowler hats became taller. They were also known as *Derbys*. For summer they were in lighter colours, being either brown or black in the winter.

Low crowned hats, also known as *wide-awakes*, had wide brims. They could be of felt or straw. Straw hats worn informally in the summer had smaller brims with a ribbon hatband, the ends of which were sometimes allowed to hang behind.

Tall-crowned top hats were one of the most popular and had many variations. The brims could be turned down front and back. The tall crowns could taper or be cylindrical. One popular style was the *Wellington hat*, typical of the 1820s, the crown curved outwards at the top.

Top hats were stiff and silk covered for formal occasions. They could be worn with frock or dress coats. By the end of Queen Victoria's reign top hats generally fell into decline.

For evening wear, however, the *gibus* top hat asd well as a cocked *chapeau bras* carried flat under the arm, remained in vogue.

By the 1870s a *deerstalker*, a type of cap, had earflaps. It was often worn in the country with Norfolk jackets or caped coats.

Stiff-crowned caps were worn for horse riding and could have a peak in the front. By the late 1830s caps made in quarters with a band, and sometimes a peak, were worn by schoolboys as well as for sports like golf, tennis and cricket.

A *Homburg* or *Trilby* hat was fashionable from the end of the century. It was of felt and the crown was indented from front to back.

Stiff silk-covered top hat, *c* 1840

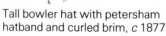

Tall bowler hat with petersham hatband and curled brim, *c* 1877

Homburg hat

High collar and bow tie, Dundreary side whiskers, *c* 1857

Hairstyles

As they had lost in popularity wigs were worn mainly by older or professional men. In the early part of the century fashionable hairstyles were short, like a Brutus crop. After about 1810 hair was grown longer allowing curls and waves to become fashionable. The back hair was generally a little shorter this being more practical with the high collars. From about 1880 hair could be brushed back and slightly raised. By the end of the century side partings became popular instead of the centre parting. Long hair was considered artistic and worn only by artists and musicians. A number of hair-care products such as macassar oil, a perfumed hair oil to keep the hairstyles sleek, as well as hair colourants, came onto the market.

Until about 1825 the face was clean shaven, but side whiskers were worn.

The new fashion was whiskers and beard to meet, framing the face. Gradually the clean-shaven look came to an end, hair slowly becoming longer with sideburns. Moustaches only became popular again around the mid 1830s when they were combed with side whiskers and a small beard beneath the chin, so as not to hide the face. In the 1850s beards became longer and bushier, as did sideburns and whiskers. Small beards, slightly pointed, were fashionable amongst the dandies.

Large whiskers known by names such as *Piccadilly weepers* or *Dundrearys* could be worn with beards or drooping moustaches. A mixture of beeswax and pomade helped stiffen the moustache.

High shirt collar with the cravat held in place with a pin. Sideburns down the side of the face were popular, *c* 1840

Wavey hairstyles, *c* 1852

Neckband tied in a bow in front, *c* 1830

High collar extending to the cheeks. The hair is worn short and curly, *c* 1823

Butterfly collar with a necktie in a large knot, *c* 1895

Hair in short curls and clean-shaven face, *c* 1834

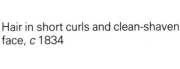

Hair brushed straight back with short whiskers and a beard, *c* 1855

Short coat with single-breasted waistcoat. The large side whiskers known as Dundrearys were worn with a drooping moustache, c 1865

Accessories

Bombast or stuffing was used at the shoulders.

Gloves for evening wear were of white silk, soft kid or suede with black stitching.

For day wear cotton, leather or wool was worn. *Muffatees* or small wrist muffs of a warm material were sometimes worn in winter for extra protection.

For evening wear *handkerchiefs* were lace trimmed and embroidered. In the 1890s they could be of silk, being only decorative, and were worn in the waistcoat pocket.

Canes were popular and made of ebony or bamboo with gold or jewelled tops. The handle could also be carved ivory.

Umbrellas with decorated handles were also popular. They had sheath covering of silk. By the 1880s they were brightly furled and if possible never unrolled as it became the fashion to use them as walking sticks.

Tie and *cravat pins*, shirt studs, rings and fobs were amongst the fashionable jewellery.

By about 1849 a short watch chain, an *Albert*, was attached to a pocket watch worn in a waistcoat pocket, with the other end secured with a bar or hook on the opposite side in a buttonhole.

A *lapel buttonhole* often carried a flower.

Eyeglasses or *monocles* were also fashionable.

Double-breasted reefer jacket. Spats are worn over shoes, c 1885

The dandy is wearing an exaggerated frock coat with wide lapels and cuffed sleeves. The waistcoat has a large roll collar. The tight fitting pantaloons are strapped under the shoes to keep them taut, c 1828

Twentieth century

The change in fashions was very slow in the twentieth century. In fact lounge jackets remained unaltered for almost a century.

The First World War was the greatest influence in the relaxing of social standards bringing strict Victorian fashions and habits to an end.

Frock coats
By the Edwardian era frock coats were almost extinct, being worn mainly for formal occasions only and, by the late 1920s, at funerals in place of morning coats. Frock coats were usually double-breasted with two or three buttons each side. Button stands were sewn to the front edges. There were buttonholes on each lapel, one to hold a flower. The lapels usually reached to the top buttons and were of the rolled variety faced with silk. The centre back vent had two buttons at the head. There could be two pockets in the back pleats with a ticket pocket in the waist seam. There could also be a breast pocket either inside or on the outside. The straight sleeves could have cuffs decorated with braid to match the coat fronts and lapel edges. If the sleeves were slit at the wrist, they had two buttons. The front and back skirts were of the same length. Frock coats were often worn open with the waistline lower than in the 1890s. Double-breasted waistcoats were frequently worn beneath the frocks, and trousers either matched or were of a striped material. Silk hats were generally worn with frock coats.

Morning coats
Morning coats were generally single-breasted with three to four buttons and high lapels early in the century; later the lapels were lowered in cut and were of the roll type. A V notch between collar and lapels became usual. In the 1920s the collars were stepped and the lapels reached the buttons. There was generally a buttonhole in the left lapel to hold a flower.

Coat fronts were cut away to slope away from the waist, the tails ending at the knees. By about 1923 the tails became a little shorter and the lapels wider. The back had a pleated central vent that ended with hip buttons. There were pockets in the pleats and an inside ticket pocket. In the 1920s flapped pockets gradually appeared. A breast pocket to hold a handkerchief was also seen from around that time.

Single-breasted morning coat with four buttons and high lapel. The trousers are striped, c 1907

Single-breasted lounge suit of flannel, worn with a waistcoat. The pockets are of the patch type. The shirt collar is high and a bow tie is worn, c 1902

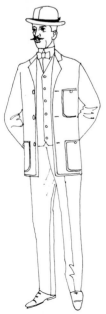

Suit with a double-breasted reefer type jacket. The pockets had welted flaps, and the trousers turn-ups. The laced shoes are in the Oxford style, *c* 1913

Single-breasted lounge suit with three buttons. The trousers had a crease down the front and had turn-ups. The high collar has stiff points and the necktie is in the form of a bow. Spats covered the top of the shoes, *c* 1914

About 1906 it became the mode to fasten the morning coats with just one or two buttons, the single link button becoming the more popular. The fronts and cuffs were frequently faced with silk or a flat braid. The sleeve cuffs could be slit ending with two buttons.

In the 1920s morning coats were lined with a black silk and cotton material, but the sleeves were generally lined in a checked shiny cotton.

Morning coats were worn mainly for formal occasions and weddings. They were generally worn with single-breasted grey waistcoats and striped grey or black trousers.

Lounge suits

By about 1902 lounge suits worn for everyday wear were usually of grey flannel or a narrow-striped material. The jackets were slightly longer than in the previous century and again had a centre seam down the back. The fronts of single-breasted jackets were slightly curved. Pockets at hip level were often flapped with a ticket pocket just above the right hand one. Breast pockets were always on the left side. Flaps could be replaced by welts or a piped edge.

Double-breasted styles usually had short, pointed lapels and a high neck with a six button fastening. The single-breasted versions had three to four buttons. The straight sleeves had slit cuffs ending with two or three buttons. About 1912 the waist was lowered slightly below the natural level and single-breasted jackets had just one or two buttons, whilst the double-breasted had two on each side.

By 1915 the jackets again became shorter and back vents and centre seams were seen less. Shaping was achieved by darts from top of the side pockets to the breast. Breast pockets again became fashionable.

Collars of the step style were usually at right angles to the lapels, that varied both in angle and size.

About 1925 lounge suits became the most popular of men's attire for all occasions. They consisted of jacket, matching waistcoat and trousers, although for casual wear trousers were of a different colour.

With the decline in wear of the more formal frock and morning coats, lounge suits were made in dark materials. Trousers were still striped. By about 1926 the waist line of lounge jackets became more defined and there were three pockets on the outside, one being a breast pocket. The ticket pocket could be on the inside or set in an outside pocket. Single-breasted jackets had roll type lapels and three buttons, with usually only the middle one fastened. The fronts were often rounded, but by 1928 square cut ones were also seen. In the 1930s the jackets became fuller over the chest, but closer fitting over the hips, and the shoulders became more squared.

Jacket sleeves were always slightly shorter than those of the shirts, so that these protruded slightly.

Reefer jackets merged in style with the lounge jackets and were usually double breasted with eight buttons. They had square cut fronts, and no central back seams.

Waistcoats

When worn with morning or frock coats, waistcoats were generally double-breasted whilst with lounge suits they were single-breasted.

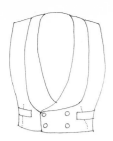

Double-breasted evening waistcoat style, c 1933

Single-breasted waistcoat, c 1933

Dinner jacket with rounded front, link button fastening and a silk faced roll collar. Over the stiff white shirt is worn a low cut double-breasted waistcoat. An Albert chain is attached to a waistcoat button with the watch in the pocket. The low pumps have a small bow decoration, c 1901

At the start of the twentieth century they were light in colour for summer, whilst for winter wear they were of patterned materials or even knitted. Later they matched the jackets. The backs were of a cheaper lining material; flannel or wool for the winter. A strap and buckle behind adjusted the waistcoat at the waist. The metal buckles were often oblong or oval in shape.

Single-breasted styles were the more popular and had a high V necked opening. Small turned down collars were not unusual at the turn of the century, but roll or step collars were also common. As the neckline became lower, collars became defunct. Waistcoats had three pockets, two at the base and one top left. Sometimes there was an extra buttonhole for the watch chain. From about 1908 of the five or six buttons, the last one was left undone, this still being the fashion today.

Double-breasted waistcoats had collars and lapels or fairly high roll collars. The styles were similar to the single-breasted waistcoats. Four or five pairs of buttons were present down the overlapping fronts. The base was fairly straight with the last button left undone.

By the late 1930s waistcoats were rarely worn in the summer.

Formal wear

Until the First World War in 1914 frock and tail coats were the correct attire for all formal occasions. They were worn with matching trousers – usually black, and white waistcoats.

Towards 1910 dinner jackets, similar to lounge jackets were becoming fashionable. They were generally single breasted with a link button instead of button and buttonhole but were often left open. The lapels were faced in silk and the collar stepped if the fronts of the jacket were square cut – if rounded roll collars were seen. Although tail coats were still worn for dinner dances into 1920s, for informal evenings dinner jackets first seen in the 1880s gained in popularity. Like lounge jackets, dinner jackets became shorter until in the early 1920s they just covered the trouser seat. In the 1930s double-breasted styles with four buttons and rolled lapels became the mode.

From the beginning of the twentieth century dress coats, generally double-breasted with cutaway fronts and two tails behind that reached the knees, were fastened with two or three buttons either side. The fronts sloped back increasingly in the early 1920s and the tails became shorter. The collar and rolling lapels were generally faced in silk. By the 1930s the shoulders became more square and lapels larger. About 1935 it was thought that midnight blue gave a darker appearance than black in artificial light.

Waistcoats worn formally could be single or double-breasts. By about 1912 the fronts were cut to form small points.

Roll collars usually had continuous lapels. The front opening was normally V shaped although U shaped openings were also fashionable. Until about 1925 white, sometimes of piqué, was fashionable than black; the backs were of a lining material, although about 1930 waistcoats were sometimes backless, being joined at the collar, with a strap and buckle at about waist level at the back.

Dinner suit, similar to a lounge suit, but in black, with a cummerband and bow tie, c 1934

Smoking jacket with Brandenburg decoration and fastenings. The roll collar and cuffs are faced in quilted silk, c 1913

Trousers followed the same trends as for everyday wear, but were always without turn-ups. In the late 1920s the outer seam had one row of braid when worn with dinner jackets and often two when worn with dress coats.

At the beginning of the twentieth century the correct attire for weddings was a frock coat with a lighter coloured waistcoat. During and after the First World War the usual dress was morning coat, waistcoat and striped trousers. Bow ties or long ties were worn with shirt wing collars. White spats and gloves, walking stick and silk top hat completed the ensemble. In the mid 1920s weddings became less formal and lounge jackets with striped trousers were seen. A flower, usually a carnation, was always worn in the lapel buttonhole, and a white handkerchief was seen about the breast pocket. Until the 1930s black frock coats, trousers and waistcoats, gloves and ties were worn at funerals. A black hatband was worn around the silk hats, and for mourning black ties and armbands were always worn. From the 1930s dark suits and black ties were worn and black armbands or diamond-shaped patches on the sleeve were worn for mourning.

Until 1937 frock coats with the fronts sloping back were worn with matching velvet breeches or trousers. Waistcoats could be black or white. Invariably white stockings were worn with black shoes on formal occasions.

For dancing, dress suits were worn and white cotton gloves were popular until the 1930s.

Informal and sportswear

Smoking jackets were still worn, similar in style to the previous century, mainly in brown or maroon. They could be worn with day or evening trousers.

Sports jackets became very popular worn mainly with flannel trousers. They were similar in style to single-breasted lounge jackets with notched lapels. They could have a back vent and three patch pockets.

Tweed *Norfolk jackets* were worn for sports with knickerbockers until the early 1920s. They were the general wear for golf until 1920 when sports jackets and breeches were worn. By about 1925 plus-fours and Fair Isle pullovers became popular, and by the 1930s trousers and shirts and ties worn under pullovers became the mode. Waist length and waterproof or suede golf jackets with waist and wrists of close-fitting knitted material became fashionable. They were fastened with buttons or a zip.

Blazers, single or double-breasted, were popular for summer wear. They usually had gilt or brass buttons and three patch pockets. They could be worn with white trousers.

Knitted *jumpers* were first worn mainly for sports. They had no fastening and were slipped over the head and known as slip-overs or sweaters. By 1912 the neckline could be lowered with the low collar or V neckline. These *pullovers*, as they were then called, when worn for a sporting club were generally in white with a band of the club colour knitted into the neck or hemline. Knitted waistcoats in various designs were replaced in the 1920s by sleeveless pullovers with V shaped necklines. Knitted cardigans, first seen in the 1890s, were like short fitted jackets with collars. They were fastened by buttons and as they became longer they could have pockets either side.

Single-breasted sports jacket worn with plus-fours and ribbed stockings, *c* 1928

Norfolk jacket worn with breeches, ribbed stockings and shoes with gaiters. The peaked cap is in eight joined pieces, *c* 1907

Stockings and cardigans were often knitted to match. For hunting black or red *frock coats* and *breeches* of cloth and later buckskin were worn with plain-topped riding boots and top hats until about 1925. *Jodhpurs* began to replace breeches and hard hats or reinforced riding caps were essential. String gloves were a popular accessory.

For shooting *tweed jackets* with gun pads on the shoulder and large pockets were worn with knickerbockers, or, as they were also known, plus-fours. Deerstalkers or tweed caps were worn with these outfits.

For cricket and tennis *white flannel trousers* and shirts were worn. Pullovers were also white with the club colours, and blazers in navy blue or black had a club badge embroidered on the top pocket. White rubber-soled canvas shoes were worn.

For headwear the cricket caps were in club colours and for tennis boaters or straw hats were worn. By the 1930s white trousers and a shirt, tie and blazer were popular. For yachting reefer jacket, cap and white canvas shoes was the usual attire and, in inclement weather, oilskins were also worn.

For swimming, at the beginning of the century, striped or plain cotton costumes in dark colours, some with half sleeves and short legs, and a rounded neckline, were worn.

By the 1920s they became sleeveless. Until the mid 1930s the back of the costume could be in a Y shape, with shoulder straps and a very narrow back piece.

After this, *bathing trunks* became acceptable.

In the early part of the twentieth century cycling outfits consisted of Norfolk jackets and knickerbockers, but as these declined in popularity when cars became more commonplace, trousers were worn instead, and cycle clips were used to prevent the bottom of the trouser legs catching on the bicycle chain or wheels.

High-necked *reefer jackets*, double breasted with small turn down collars, yachting caps, and gloves were worn for motoring. Leather or fur-lined coats being worn for the winter. As cars became more commonplace the need for special clothes ceased.

In the late 1920s ski outfits consisted of waterproof breeches and oiled stockings and gloves. Thick woollen sweaters were knitted to match caps and scarves.

Outdoor wear

Coats in general were slightly waisted and darted at the breast for a better shape. They were often closed with a fly front and had a vent at the back.

At the beginning of the century, for a very short time, top frock coats similar to frocks, but longer and double breasted, were worn without jackets beneath. Still the most popular of coats was the *Chesterfield* or *Chester*, single or double-breasted. By about 1923 it was mainly double-breasted with four to six buttons, a velvet collar and three outside pockets, but by the end of the 1920s the coat was shorter, to calf length.

Ulsters were still similar in style to the previous period, worn mainly for travelling and country wear. They were made in a warmer material than other coats.

Covert coats, shorter than Ulsters, single breasted and fly fronted, had raglan sleeves and sometimes side vents. They were worn on informal

Double-breasted Ulster worn over a typical riding outfit of the 1900s

Swimsuit with a belted waist, *c* 1929

The shooting outfit consisting of Norfolk jacket and matching knickerbockers. The cape and cap are also in matching checks. The brogues are worn with knee high gaiters, *c* 1900

Single-breasted Chesterfield. The striped trousers are peg-topped and the spats fastened at the sides and held under the shoes with straps, *c* 1920

Caped Ulster coat, *c* 1900

Ulster style with patch pockets and a belt, *c* 1936

Raglan fly-fronted coat, *c* 192

'Bond Street' scarf, c 1902

'Court' collar, c 1900

'Admiral' collar, c 1900

'Whitehall' collar, c 1900

'Westminster' cravat, c 1902

Evening bow tie, c 1902

occasions and were popular as motoring coats.

Raglan coats were still the same as in the nineteenth century. Rubberised cotton raincoats were popular. A new style created by the First World War, was a trench coat. This had double-yoked shoulders and was belted.

Capes and coats with split capes or wings were still worn early in the 1900s.

Neckwear

Shirt collars were separate from shirts and attached with collar studs, held in place in the front by two buttonholed tabs attached to a stand in the front, beneath the tie.

At the beginning of the century collars were about 3 in. (8 cm) high and stiffened with starch. There were several styles, such as a stand-fall (also known as a double collar) and a single stand or winged collar with the fronts pointed down. The winged collars were worn mainly with evening dress. By about 1912 the height of collars decreased from between 3 in. to 3½ in. to between 1½ in. to 2½ in. (8 cm to 9 cm to between 4 cm to 6 cm).

By about 1930 separate and attached collars became softer, the double collar being the most popular.

Celluloid collar stiffeners were inserted betwen a double piece of material at the points.

There were varous kinds of neckties, bow ties being one of the most popular. For evening wear they were mainly in white piqué, but by 1914 black was also worn with dinner wear.

Long ties, known as *four-in-hands*, were tied in a slip knot, and had square or pointed ends. They could be in plain or patterned designs, diagonal stripes being popular in school, club or regimental colours.

At the beginning of the century ties with the knot in front ready-made and fastened at the back were worn. Bow ties could also be bought, fastening at the back with an adjustable buckle and strap.

Legwear

Knickerbockers worn with woollen stockings were still popular in the first part of the twentieth century, mainly for sports. They were loose and fastened at the knee with a band, buckled or buttoned. Just prior to the First World War they became even wider and were known as plus-fours.

Trousers were generally narrow with a crease down the front, Lounge suit trousers often had turn-ups, and these styles were slightly shorter, just reaching the top of the shoes.

About 1912 peg-topped trousers again became popular and were made in the same way as in the mid-nineteenth century. As trousers became wider turn-ups were less often seen, but by the 1920s trousers again became narrower, again becoming wider, until by 1925 they became very baggy and were known as *Oxford* bags. When this fashion declined trousers were made to fit better than previously and had two pleats in the waistband. They were made to fit to just over the instep.

From the mid 1920s striped trousers were worn with formal jackets. Informal flannels from about 1922 had side straps and loops instead of brace buttons on the waistband. The loose adjustable straps had a

At their most extreme Oxford bags were 47 in. (120 cm) wide at the bottom of each leg. The front of the single-breasted jacket are rounded and a flower is worn in the lapel buttonhole. The shirt collar is rounded and the tie is a four-in-hand, one of the most popular knots. A waistcoat is also worn, *c* 1927

Suspender worn around the calf to hold up the sock

Golfing shoes, *c* 1922

Low boot laced and a tab at the back for easier putting on, *c* 1924

buttonhole which fastened to a button attached to the band. Belts could also be threaded through loops at the waistband and could be of self material or leather. The waistband was sometimes made to extend on the left and closed with a metal hook to a bar on the opposite side.

Instead of buttons and fly fronts, zip fasteners were beginning to make their appearance in the mid 1930s.

Footwear

At the beginning of the 1900s low boots were popular in the winter whilst laced shoes were worn in the summer.

The boots were fastened with buttons or laces and often had a tab at the back. The heels were fairly low. The slightly rounded toe pieces could be of cloth or suede. A popular style of shoe was the *co-respondent*; the toe caps and the part at the back were of a contrasting colour, usually brown and white or dark red and white, to the remainder. The toe caps could be decorated with punched holes. Elegant shoes were often in white buckskin, another popular colour was light tan or yellow as it was also called.

When the shoes became more square, they were known as Bulldog toes. *Brogues* were also popular from about 1918. They were made fashionable by the Prince of Wales and had fringed tongues. By the 1930s they became a more robust style, being worn more for walking and country wear.

Oxford type shoes were more popular amongst younger men at first they were of plain patent leather with a four-holed lace fastening. Varying types of leather as well as the improvements in shoemaking allowed shoes to be made in better designs. Black and brown laced shoes of suede or leather were very popular from the 1930s. They could also have high tongues with a strap and buckle fastening.

For dancing and evening wear *pumps*, low-cut in the front, remained in fashion. *Sandals* and sports shoes in canvas with rubber soles were worn from the 1920s.

Rubber Wellington boots or *galoshes*, a type of overshoe fitting over walking shoes, were worn in inclement weather.

Spats were still popular until about 1939. They were generally of drill or felt, covering the tops of shoes and the ankles. They buttoned on the outside and were held down under the shoe with elastic or strap and buckle. Light colours such as beige, grey or white were the most fashionable.

Gaiters were also worn and were similar to spats, but reached the calf and were worn for outdoor sports.

Socks were clocked and held up with *garters* or suspenders above the knees.

Co-respondent shoe in contrasting colours. The lacing is over a tongue, *c* 1938

Hand-sewn shoe in box calf, *c* 1927

Folding opera hat known as a 'gibus', c 1902

Homburg 1920s

Soft trilby with brim turned down all round, c 1927

Boater with a wide hatband, c 1913

Homburg style with a crown indented front to back and a ribbed hatband. The brim is bound in silk, c 1917

Silk top hat, c 1921

Soft trilby hat, c 1939

Small brimmed bowler hat with hatband, c 1935

Headwear

Tweed hats and caps as well as deerstalkers were still being worn at the beginning of the twentieth century. Before the First World War some type of headwear was always worn out of doors. For formal occasions, day or evening, black silk top hats were worn. After that time they were just worn for weddings and race meetings in a grey cloth. For evening wear a *Gibus* or opera hat was still worn. It was collapsible, the crown being supported by a spiral spring and enclosed in the lining.

Bowler or *Derby* hats, fairly flat with curved brims, were usual wear. Other styles included *Trilbys* and *Homburgs*. Homburgs were of a stiffer felt than Trilbys which could also be of a velour or straw for summer, but were otherwise very similar with the turned up brim bound in silk and the crown indented from front to back.

By the 1930s both bowlers and Homburgs were worn less, being replaced by a black Trilby style known as an *Anthony Eden* hat, after the politician, and worn by businessmen as well as formally. The dented crown became more rounded, the sides could be indented slightly when the hats were made of a softer felt.

Light-weight *panama* or straw hats were wide brimmed, worn in the summer. *Boaters* were also popular.

Hairstyles

Hair styles altered very little in the early 1900s, centre partings being popular until about 1905. Gradually hair was cut shorter at the back and sides, and was kept flat with hair cream and oils. Slightly raised hair in front – the Pompadour – was popular until about 1930.

By the late 1930s there was no parting in the hair, the hair being brushed straight back so that the contour of the head was seen. The hair could be brushed at the temples to form slightly raised wings.

About 1934 permanent waving for men became acceptable. Hair pieces and toupées to match the existing hair had been worn by balding men for some time.

Large waxed moustaches were fashionable until the 1920s, after which time beards and moustaches declined in popularity.

During the First World War a toothbrush moustache became popular – this was typified by two very different personalities – Charlie Chaplin, the little man with aspirations but but no prospects and Adolf Hitler with his mad lust for power. About 1935 beards and moustaches again became the mode in similar styles to those of early 1900s.

Sleeveless V-necked pullover, all the edges ribbed for firmer support, *c* 1932

V-necked slipover with short sleeves worn over an open-necked shirt. The trousers with turn-ups are pleated at the waist, *c* 1936

Accessories

When moustaches were in fashion, moustache cups were made with a chin guard or bridge to support the moustache and prevent it from getting wet when drinking.

Hair was curled and waved with curling irons in the early part of the century.

Mud packs were used to smooth the skin and draw out blemishes. To smell sweet and clean toilet waters or scented hair tonics were used. Aftershave, creams and powders became popular in the late 1920s and 1930s. Early in the century a little rouge could be applied to pale cheeks or a lighter coloured powder for high cheek colouring.

Gloves for day wear were of leather, suede or cloth, whilst for evenings they were of a soft kid. Motoring gloves were of cotton or silk with leather for the palms. Gloves were generally fastened at the back of the wrists with one or two buttons.

By the 1930s gloves were not an essential accessory except for driving when they were of string or leather.

With the growing popularity of an outside breast pocket, *handkerchiefs*, usually white with a coloured border, were seen to protrude slightly.

Umbrellas became more popular than walking sticks or canes. They were tightly furled and the handles in various shapes, the crook being one of the most popular. They could be made in jointed cane, or were leather covered.

When *canes* or walking sticks were carried they often had recesses in the handles to carry small items such as a pipe, cigarettes or matches.

Pocket watches were worn until the decline of dress coats when wrist watches, first seen just before the First World War, became standard. These had leather straps, the watch being either square or oblong.

Tie pins often had ornamental jewels or a design at the head and fastened ties to the shirts with either a safety pin device or a clip.

Collar studs and cuff links were made to match and for evening wear also matched the buttons on the waistcoats. They were often of gold with mother-of-pearl facings.

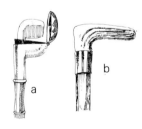

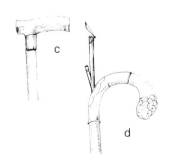

Various types of stick handle tops: (a) Silver-handled stick, the top used as a pipe holder, (b) Stag-horn handle, (c) Ivory top, (d) The top held ten cigarettes and a matchbox, all *c* 1902

Glossary of Terms

Bagwig   Powdered and the back tied into a black bag

Banjan   Loose informal morning jacket

Blazer   Single- or double-breasted informal jacket with three patch pockets and metal buttons

Boater   Stiff straw hat with flat crown and a brim

Bow tie   Necktie with a bow in front

Bowler hat   Hard felt with a domed crown and narrow turned-up brim

Box pleat   Parallel pleats to form a box shape

Braces   Straps to hold up trousers or breeches, passing over the shoulders

Braes   Loose fitting drawers, tied with a running string. Ankle length until the eleventh century, then shorter to the knees

Breeches   Upper part of long hose combined with a form of tights, a different colour until the sixteenth century. Later – leg coverings ending at the knees

Brogue   Heavy shoe with punched-out design on the uppers

Buskins   High boots reaching the knees

Button stand   Separate pieces of material – one with buttons, the other with buttonholes, sewn to the front of garments to take the strain

Cardigan   Casual jacket of knitted material, buttoning down the front.

Cassock   Long loose overcoat, buttoning from neck to hem

Caul   Net foundation for wigs

Chapeau bras   Tricorne hat, usually carried flat under the arm

Chaperon   Hood with liripipe, twisted up or left hanging

Chemise   Undergarment

Chesterfield   Knee length overcoat with a fly front

Chiton   Greek rectangular piece of material sewn up the sides and fastened at the shoulder

Clocks   Decoration on side of socks or stockings

Clogs   Wooden soled overshoes

Codpiece   Small bag concealing front opening of breeches, also used as a pocket

Coif   Close fitting linen cap

Copotain   High crowned cone shaped hat with a small brim

Corespondent shoes   Two-tone, tan or brown and white toecap and backpiece of a different colour and possibly material

Cote-hardie   Close fitting knee length overgarment buttoned down the front. Elbow length sleeves with long extensions.

Covert coat   Short fly fronted with side vents

Cowl   Hood attached to a cape

Cut-away   Single-breasted coat with skirts cut away in front, the back reaching the knees

Dart   Pointed tuck of material sewn together for better fit

Deerstalker   Tweed cap with earflaps tied over the crown or worn around the ears

Dinner jacket   Informal with roll collar and lapels to waist edged in silk or satin, with cuffed sleeves

Double breasted   Overlapping fronts with a double row of buttons, one as decoration and the other practical

Doublet   Padded jacket, close fitting and waisted

Fall   Buttoned front fastening of trousers or breeches, kind of flap

Farthingale   Structure of shaped hoops to distend sleeves

Fly   Strip of material concealing buttons and buttonhole fastenings

Frock coat   As tail coat, buttoned to waist with a back vent and side pleats

Frogging   Looped braid fastening

Gaiters   Ankle covering top of shoes or boots, fastened on the outside and held down with elastic or strap

Galoshes   Protective overshoes

Garde corps   Voluminous supertunic with long wide sleeves and a hood

Garters   Strip of material sometimes elasticated to hold up stockings

Gibus   Collapsible top hat

Gipon   Close fitting and padded jacket to knee level in the 14th Century, later becoming shorter with long tight sleeves

Hanging sleeve   Long sleeve, slit in the upper half for arm to protrude

Herigaud   Three-quarter to full length gown with hanging sleeves

Hessians   Calf length riding boots decorated with a tassel

Highlows   Ankle boots, fastening in front

Homburg   Stiff felt hat with bound brim curved at sides and crown indented from front to back

Houppelande   Voluminous gown falling in folds from shoulder to ground with very wide sleeves

Jackboots   Black leather knee high boots with broad heels

Jacket   Short body garment, an outer garment after about 1450

Jerkin   Worn over a doublet, sometimes with hanging sleeves

Knickerbockers   Loose breeches to just below knees,

gathered to a band

Lapel   Turned-back upper part of front of a jacket or coat

Liripipe   Long hanging part of a chaperon or hood

Lounge jacket   Short skirted, slightly waisted, usually had rounded corners

Mandilion   Loose fitting hip length jacket with open sides

M or V notch   Cut in shape of M or V between collar and lapel

Morning coat   Like a riding coat sometimes known as a Newmarket. Fronts sloping away from the waist with a back vent

Negligée   Informal attire

Netherstocks   Lower part of hose

Norfolk jacket   With box pleats, front and back. Patch pockets and belt of self material. Yoke added about 1894 from which pleats eminated

Opera hat   Soft crowned high hat, could be folded between the side brims, forerunner of the gibus

Oxford Bags   Trousers with extremely wide flared bottoms

Oxford shoes   High vamped lace-up shoes

Panama hat   Straw hat made of plaited fibre

Pantaloons   Close fitting shaped tights – slit at the sides by the ankles

Partlet   Sleeveless jacket – fill-in for a low décolletage

Patent leather   Specially treated and varnished to give a high shine

Patten   Wooden platform soles to keep footwear raised from dirty roads

Pea jacket   As reefer or pilot coat, usually with large buttons

Peascod   Padding in front to give a protruding bulge over doublet girdle

Peg-topped trousers   Wide at waist, tightening towards the ankles

Petasos   Greek, straw or felt flat crowned hat with broad brim, held on with string under the chin

Petticoat, Petticote   Undergarment similar to a doublet, padded for warmth, later like a waistcoat

Phrygian bonnet   Made of felt or leather and fastened under the chin in Roman times. Later woollen cap with turned down points

Pilot coat   Double-breasted, wide-lapelled short overcoat, sometimes with a velvet collar

Piqué   Raised rib or honeycomb effect cotton material

Plus-fours   Voluminous breeches to the knees, plus four inches

Points   Ties or decorative bunches of ribbon bows

Pumps   Thin low sided shoes worn on formal occasions, sometimes with ribbon bow decoration. Also worn for dancing

Queue   Hanging tail of wig

Raglan sleeve   Sewn from underarm to neck without a shaped armhole

Reefer   Short top coat or jacket, usually double breasted

Revers   Turned-back edge of coat or jacket

Roll collar   Turned over collar continuous with lapels

Roquelaure   Full cape with cape collar, buttoning in front and a vent at the back, usually for horse riding

Rowels   Spiked revolving disc at end of spurs

Ruff   Circular collar gathered at neck or at wrist

Side bodies   Separate panel inserted between underarm seams to give a better fit

Silk hat   Like a top hat

Single breasted   Single row of buttons fastening a coat or jacket which does not overlap in front

Slops   Wide knee breeches ending loosely just above the knees

Spattersashes   Leggings extending over the feet fastened in the outside and strapped beneath

Spats   Similar to short gaiters and spatterdashes, buttoned down one side

Spencer   Short waistlength jacket buttoned in front

Stand collar   Collar without turn-over

Step   Gap between collar and lapel

Stock   High stiffened neck cloth

Stomacher   Front chest piece covering the low fronted garment

Supertunic   Loose garment worn over tunic with wide sleeves – also called a surcote

Surtout   Overcoat, long and loose with caped collar in the 18th century, and similar to a frock coat in the 19th

Taglioni frock   Single-breasted with short full skirts, collar and cape or lapels

Top boots   Reaching just below knees with contrasting turn-over

Top hat   Tall high crowned with narrow brim

Tricorne   Three cornered cocked hat

Trilby   Soft felt hat

Turn-ups   Base of trousers turned up

Ulster   Overcoat with a half or complete belt

Upperstocks   Breeches or seat part of hose

Vent   Short slit from hem upwards

Venetians   Pear shaped knee breeches with bombast around the hips

Waistcoat   sleeveless jacket, usually worn beneath outer jackets

Welt   Strengthened edge of garment

Wing collar   High and stiff with turned back corners

Wings   Stiff crescent shaped bands over shoulder seams

Bibliography

Amphlett, Hilda, *Hats*, Sadler 1974

Asser, Joyce, *Historic Hairdressing*, Pitman 1966

Barfoot, A, *Everyday Costume in Britain*, Batsford 1961

Binder, Pearl, *Muffs and Morals*, Harrap 1953

Blum, S, *Everyday Fashions of the '20s*, Dover 1981

Boehn, M von, *Modes and Manners* (8 vols), Harrap 1926-35

Bott, A, *Our Fathers*, Heinemann 1931

Boucher, F, *20,000 Years of Fashion*, Abrams

Bradfield, N, Historical Costumes of England, Harrap 1972

Braun and Schneider, *Historic Costume in Pictures*, Dover 1975

Brooke, Iris, *History of English Costume*, Methuen 1972

Calthrop, D C, *English Costume*, A & C Black 1906

Cassin-Scott, J, *Costume and Fashion 1550-1760*, Blandford 1975

Casin-Scott, J, *Costume and Fashion 1760-1920*, Blandford 1971

Clinch, George, *English Costume*, E P Publishing 1975

Contini, M, *Fashion*, Crescent 1965

Cunnington, C W and P and Beard, *Dictionary of English Costume*, A and C Black 1972

Cunnington, C W and P, *Handbook of English Mediaeval Costume*, Faber 1969

Cunnington, C W and P, *Handbook of English Costume in the 16th Century*, Faber 1970

Cunnington, C W and P, *Handbook of English Costume in the 17th Century*, Faber 1974

Cunnington, C W and P, *Handbook of English Costume in the 18th Century*, Faber 1964

Cunnington, C W and P, *Handbook of English Costume in the 19th Century*, Faber 1970

Cunnington, C W and P, *Handbook of English Costume in the 20th Century*, Faber 1975

Davenport, M, *The Book of Costume*, Crown 1972

De Anfrasio, Charles and Roger, *History of Hair*, Bonanza 1970

Fairholt, F W, *Costume in England*, Chapman & Hall 1846

Fairholt, F W, *Glossary of Costume in England*, E P Publishing 1976

Garland, Madge, *History of Fashion*, Orbis 1975

Gorsline, D, *what People Wore*, Bonanza

Hansen, H, *Costume Cavalcade*, Methuen 1956

Harrison, Molly, *Hairstyles and Hairdressing*, Ward Lock 1968

Harter, J, *Men – Pictoral Archives*, Dover 1980

Hill, G, *History of English Dress*, (2 vols), Bentley 1893

Kohler, C, *History of Costume*, Dover 1963

Laver, James, *Costumes through the Ages*, Thames and Hudson 1964

Laver, James, *Concise History of Costume*, Thames and Hudson 1969

Laver, James, *Modesty in Dress*, Heinemann 1969

Laver, James, *Dandies*, Weidenfeld & Nicolson 1968

Lister, Margot, *Costume*, Jenkins 1967

Norris, Herbert, *Costume and Fashion*, Dent 1924

Pistolese and Horstig, *History of Fashions*, Wiley 1970

Planche, J R, *British Costume*, C Cox 1847

Selbie, R, *Anatomy of Costume*, Mills and Boon 1977

Stibbert, F, *Civil and Military Clothing in Europe*, Benjamin Blom 1968

Strutt, J, *Complete View of the Dress and Habits of the People of England* (2 vols), Bohn 1842

Truman, N, *Historic Costuming*, Pitman 1956

Waugh, Norah, *The Cut of Men's Clothes 1600-1930*, Faber 1964

Wilcox, R T, *Dictionary of Costume*, Batsford 1970

Wilson, E, *History of Shoe Fashions*, Pitman 1974

Yarwood, D, *Outline of English Costume*, Batsford 1967

Yarwood, D, *Encylopaedia of World Costume*, Batsford 1978

Yarwood, D, *English Costume from the 2nd Century BC to the Present Day* Batsford 1975

Pictorial Encyclopedia of Fashion, Hamlyn 1968

Index